MENTAL WELFARE COMMISSIC

Guardianship IN SCOTLAND

HUW RICHARDS · CHRISTINE McGREGOR
EDINBURGH · HMSO

© Crown copyright 1992.
Applications for reproduction should be
made to HMSO.
First published 1992.

ISBN 0 11 494197 1

Foreword

The Mental Welfare Commission has had a long history of involvement in the monitoring and oversight of statutory provision for the guardianship of mentally disordered people reaching back to the original Lunacy Act of 1859.

The period preceding the 1984 Act was marked by three Commission publications relating to guardianship issues and under the Chairmanship of my predecessor, Mr Peter Millar, the Commission's interest was continued with the decision to produce a contemporary publication.

Commissioners have an active concern with trends in social policy provision relating to guardianship, its history and development as well as its application in current practice to individual cases.

The Commission visits all people subject to guardianship, considers matters of case review and regularly discusses issues arising with local authorities. It is therefore appropriate at this time with the recent publication of the Scottish Law Commission's Discussion Paper 94, Mentally Disabled Adults, that we should make publicly available our knowledge of guardianship in Scotland.

Huw Richards and Christine McGregor are to be congratulated on a most thorough and comprehensive study of the subject which I am confident will be of interest and value to all those involved in this area.

HAZEL J ARONSON Q.C.
Chairman

Acknowledgements

The authors would like to thank professional colleagues at the Commission for their assistance in undertaking parts of the work and in particular the valuable contribution made by Dr Connaughton, Dr Lyall, Dr Weatherhead in the completion of the questionnaires and Commissioners, Donald Macdonald and Robert Davis for their helpful commentary on the text.

HUW RICHARDS
HM Social Work Commissioner

CHRISTINE McGREGOR
Social Work Officer

Contents

CHAPTER 1
Page **History of Guardianship**
The Historical Background
Early Origins
Guardianship of Children
The Poor Law
Boarding Out
Reports of General Board of Commissioners in Lunacy for Scotland, General Board of Control, Mental Welfare Commission
The Review of Mental Health Acts, 1959 and 1960
The Mental Health (Scotland) Act 1984
Summing up the Historical Background

CHAPTER 2
Page **The Contemporary Literature on Guardianship**
The "Unpopularity" of Guardianship
The Welfare Grounds
Guardianship and the Elderly
Guardianship and Offenders
Practice Issues
Guardianship and Community Treatment Orders
Conclusion

CHAPTER 3
Page **Survey of Guardianship**
Introduction
Section 1: General Information
Who are Guardians?
Who is subject to Guardianship?
Gender
Age
Location of Cases
Local Authority Guardians; "named" Guardians; the role of Mental Health Officers; statutory visiting and Care Management
Duration of Guardianship
Are people on Guardianship subject to other measures of care or control?
Where do people on Guardianship live and with whom?
Summary

Contents (continued)

Section 2: Problems Experienced by People Subject to Guardianship
Finance
Family Relationships
Vulnerability
Occupational/Recreational
Behavioural problems
Mental Health; Handicap; Illness, Dementia and General Health Problems
Education
Housing/Accommodation
Interpersonal and Sexual problems
Hygiene and Clothing problems
Summary of problems reported for people subject to Guardianship

Section 3: Grounds Presented to the Court on Application or Renewal
Section 4: Powers of Guardians
Section 5: Services Received by People on Guardianship
Section 6: Management of Funds
Section 7: Court Hearings. Orders for Discharge and Complaints

CHAPTER 4 Conclusions and Future Trends
Page
Historical background and Survey
The Local Authority as Guardian
Placement and Costs of Care
Care, Control and Risk
Practice Guidance
Case Management
Personal Guardianship
Fund Management
Criteria for Guardianship: Incapacity and Welfare
Conclusion

CHAPTER 1

The Historical Background

The history of guardianship is not recorded in any systematic way and can be discerned as a theme, mainly from study of works devoted to other subjects such as Poor Law, Lunacy and Mental Disorder Legislation, Reports for Parliament and general Social Welfare. It follows that any student of guardianship has to consider the interplay of different social factors and legal developments over the years, if not centuries, to reach some understanding of the present situation. The background however is complex - it does not unfold in any neat way and this brief historical study attempts only to follow trends of use and views on guardianship, mostly through past Mental Welfare Commission records.

From earliest times attitudes towards people judged to be mentally disordered - to use the contemporary term - have varied and have been defined by diverse aspects of religious beliefs, economic strategies, psychological forces, political stances, reformers' zeal and so on. The demon-possessed, witches, the mad, those of "furious mind", the insane have figured in society and evoked responses. One discernible element throughout recorded history has been conflict between concepts of care and control. Compassion for the deranged is evident in the Bible, Plato's Laws proposed heavy fines for anyone who neglected to care for a mad slave, village communities contained their idiots, the wandering imbecile could expect a seat at the poorest of tables, food was taken to the hermit in his cave. At times the care has been meagre and the control excessive, as best illustrated by the burning of witches during the 16th, 17th and 18th centuries throughout Europe; both however have survived as characteristics of responses to mental disorder down through the ages. The theme of the shifting balance of caring and controlling in relation to those afflicted is significant in the evolving of guardianship systems.

Early Origins

The origins of guardianship appear to be more in relation to care of property rather than of person, although the ancient concept of "parens patriae" inferred State protection for those who could not care for themselves. Also Roman Law as early as the 5th century BC reveals guardianship of a sort in The Twelve Tables. "If a person is a fool, let the person and his goods be under the protection of his family or his paternal relatives, if he is not under the care of anyone". This very firmly gave control and presumably the duty of protection, to the head of the family.

English Statute makes first mention of a form of guardianship in Statute de Prerogativa Regis[1] (concerning the prerogatives of the King) about 1300 AD, which powered the Crown to take over for life the estates of "natural fools". Interestingly enough the Statute made distinction between "natural fools" and those who "happen to fail of wit"; the latter group being given the benefit of a return of their property should "they come to right mind". In effect the King could seize the land of an "idiot" and yet have no duty to maintain the person or his family, until death restored the property to the rightful heirs. Clearly the De Prerogativa Regis was proprietorial in essence and as such remained in effect for some 600 years until Lunacy Law was enacted. Practically every commentator on guardianship of the person remarks that historically Guardianship Law has been almost exclusively concerned with property management to the neglect of personal protection.[2]

Guardianship of Children

An area which appears to have some developmental parallels to guardianship of mentally disorder persons over the years, is the wardship of children. There is certainly some shared language and the index reference to guardianship in many books of past eras often turns out to be in relation to "minors" not "lunatics". To some extent this continues into modern times and in attempting to make international comparisons of guardianship, one has to clarify what is being meant by the term.

Commentaries on social history[3] show that systems of wardship/ guardianship for children developed gradually from Roman times onwards across Europe. Earliest Germanic Law had a known guardianship exercised by kin to orphaned child and the Franks were prepared to give to the King a theoretical duty of protecting orphans. Mary Bateson[4] writing on the development of Borough Court customs claims that the practice of the Franks was the source from which these Courts first derived power to appoint a guardian when no natural one existed and ultimately their control of the selection of guardians in all cases.

The development of guardianship in respect of children shows the movement from legitimate guardianship (the right of kin to claim or be compelled to accept guardianship) to dative guardianship where the Court granted the guardianship to an appointed person. There is also evidence of control of guardianship by oversight of King, Feudal Lord or community - at least in respect of cases where the ward had "wealth and chattels". Moreover as the years passed, notions of child protection began to feature by the including of care of the person as well as control of goods and property.

The parallels between protective treatment of and legislation for children and those for the mentally disordered are tentative but there are some examples. Historical evidence shows that wardship similar to that provided for children with bequests of land, was applied to adult persons of unsound mind[5]. The Report of the Royal Lunacy Commission for Scotland of 1857 describes the early Court procedure of appointing Tutors-at-Law for the care of the person affirmed to be a lunatic and the protection of his property and goes on to say "The powers of the Tutor-in-Law to lunatics.... are precisely analogous to those of Tutors-at-Law to minors". Also it may not be too fanciful to claim that the Poor Law boarding-out arrangements for "needy" children underwrote the development of that protective service in respect of pauper lunatics through both systems being the responsibility of the Inspectors of Poor and their parish masters. Adrian Ward writing in contemporary times on Scots Law in relation to persons with mental handicap[6] contends that the Law of children and of the mentally handicapped "share similar concepts and terminology" and claims that

> "there has been a tendency for aspects of the Law of the mentally handicapped to be stated by referring to equivalent concepts in the Law of children";

and the Royal Commission of 1954-1957 arguing that Local Health Authorities should be able to act as guardians of mentally disordered persons said

> "This would be analogous to their duty to act as a 'fit person' under the Children and Young Persons Acts".

Finally guardians appointed under the Mental Health (Scotland) Act 1960 had the powers of a parent over a "pupil" child.

Guardianship

The Poor Law

The precursor of Lunacy Law was Poor Law and the fate of mentally afflicted people was inextricably bound up with Statutes dealing predominantly with their poverty rather than their illness. Early legislation dealing with the poor was inspired however less by a desire to relieve poverty than by an effort to get rid of rogues and beggars and certainly many of the lunatics of the time came into the latter category if not the former.

The first Poor Law Act of 1424 allowed persons between 14 and 70 years of age to beg, if unable to gain a living otherwise. The Act of 1503 amended the previous Act to restrict begging to "crukit folk, blind folk, impotent folk and waik folk"[7]. Over the centuries until the Poor Law Act of 1845, a system of parish relief for the "deserving" poor and punishment of vagabonds persisted; pauper lunatics fell to manage as best they could within the very variable exercise of this legislation.

The 1845 Poor Law Act was significant in our terms, because it introduced a Board of Supervision and required the appointment of an executive in the Inspector of Poor. He was also to become the local executive officer under the Lunacy Acts, the first of which became Statute 12 years later in 1857. The Inspector of Poor may be seen as one of the earliest predecessors of today's Mental Health Officers[8]. He was however predominantly an official arbiter of parochial relief and his initial concern with the insane was the extent to which they were chargeable to public funds. The methods of disposal open to him were placement in the "new" asylums, Poor Houses or private boarding-out establishments. His prime concern had to be costs and the cheaper rates of Poor House residence often weighed decisively against commital to an asylum.

Parochial Boards obtained licences for parts of the Poor Houses to become lunatic wards in direct opposition to transferring persons to asylums, one of the provisions of the first Lunacy Act in 1857. Also the development of boarding-out lunatics in private establishments can be seen to have come about as another cheaper alternative in the controversy about custodial care locations. Mackay in his 1907 book on Scottish Poor Law[9] states

> "an Inspector of Poor can do a great deal to save expense on lunatics chargeable to his parish in an asylum, by constantly making enquiries as to

whether any of these lunatics are suitable for being boarded-out in a private dwelling".

Boarding-out

Scotland is viewed internationally as having been one of the pioneers of the boarding-out system. G A Tucker writing "Lunacy in Many Lands" in 1887 stated

> "the experiment of boarding-out single pauper patients is one which has only been tried in Scotland and in Belgium - on a small and circumscribed scale in the former country and in a very large way at Gheel in the latter, where a veritable lunatic colony has been established. The boarding-out system, as a system, presents many advantages, but its application requires great care and circumspection. So far as it has been adopted in Scotland it has given satisfaction to the lunacy authorities, and seems to be entirely successful".

The Royal Commission on the Care and Control of the Feeble-minded, 1908 recommended that

> "the system of boarding-out or family guardianship, as practised in Scotland, should be adopted in England for suitable cases".

As already mentioned, Section 95 of the Lunacy Act of 1857 contained a provision to the effect that all pauper lunatics must be removed to the Lunacy District Asylum unless the newly-created General Board of Lunacy in Scotland sanctioned their disposal otherwise. It was this provision which brought the Board into official relationship with all pauper lunatics wherever placed and which enabled them to permit placement in private dwellings. The conditions under which patients were established in this mode of care were closely described and involved medical certification, an application to the Board of Lunacy and the assurance that

> "the circumstances in which the patient will be placed are suitable and sufficient for his proper care and treatment".

Patients so placed had to be visited at least once a year by a Board's Commissioner, and the Inspector of Poor, who was usually instrumental in identifying a suitable guardian (the word used), had to visit half-yearly. Finally a local Medical Officer had to visit quarterly and the local visits had to be recorded in a visiting book kept in the patient's home. A case record was kept at the office of the Board of Lunacy. The Royal Commission on the Care and Control of the Feeble-Minded, 1908 commented

> "The diffusion of this method of family guardianship in Scotland is very remarkable. Though only of comparatively recent origin, it is now very well established and works smoothly and satisfactorily".

They quote Mr Motion, Inspector of Poor to the Parish of Glasgow

> "Previous to May 1885, the Borough and Parish of Glasgow had practically no boarding-out. After that period, to prevent the erection of additions to the asylums, and as we knew there were a number of chronic harmless cases 'fit to be boarded-out', efforts were at once started to find suitable places".

Mr Motion goes on to describe his early efforts to find boarding-out places in Fife, finishing by saying

> ".... After the first few, we could then pick and choose the best type of guardian".

Thus the 1857 Lunacy Act provided Statute for the boarding-out of insane people under specified terms of control and supervision. In addition it allowed for a system of payment to carers for the services given.

Arthur Mitchell, Deputy Commissioner in Lunacy for Scotland, writing in 1864[10] on the insane in private dwellings described his object as:

> 1. to exhibit the condition of the insane in private dwellings; and

> 2. to show the extent of proper treatment which can be found in private dwellings for a certain class of the insane, and the necessity which exists for providing, for the accumulation of chronic cases in asylums, an outlet which shall meet the requirements of humanity and economy.

Dr Mitchell based his book on the experience of 2,508 visits having been paid to insane persons in private dwellings by the Board and came out with a view firmly in favour of the boarding-out system and its extension on two grounds.

"1. It is the best thing for these patients.

2. It is the best thing for the country."

He went on to say that a recent amendment in the Lunacy Law allowing the special licensing without fee, of dwellings to house up to 4 lunatics, would facilitate the extending of the boarding-out scheme.

Some 30 years later, Dr Sutherland, Deputy Commissioner in Lunacy reporting in 1897 on the same subject endorses the success of the system.

"To have had in Scotland, for well nigh 40 years, on an average more than 2,000 insane poor, residing with respectable families, in quiet, decayed Scottish villages and rural districts and sharing to the full, or to a large extent, the family life of the house, and to some extent that of the community and to have no untoward accident occur, save one, is striking testimony to the success of the system whether regarded in the interests 1. of the insane themselves; 2. of the guardians who board them, and whose means of subsistence is thereby supplemented; and 3. of the taxpayer. That it is a boon to the taxpayer, is evident when it is shown that the cost roughly speaking, is one-half of that required for asylum maintenance.....".

Dr Sutherland goes on to say:

"but the system has more than economy to commend it. Colonial, European, and American specialists have been commissioned by their respective governments to visit Scotland in order to see the modus operandi, and these have returned with such favourable accounts that other nations are following suit".

Dr Sutherland's material which appeared in 2 articles in the Poor Law Magazine[11] showed the procedures required for boarding-out in private dwellings to have similarities with present day guardianship. The Inspector of Poor had to submit an application accompanied by 2 medical certificates to the General Board of Lunacy.

"If the General Board is satisfied as to the suitability of the patient, the guardian, the dwelling and the locality, the arrangement is ratified".

Reference has already been made to the statutory visit requirements and central supervision by the General Board of Lunacy was required. Guardians were selected and supported by the Inspector of Poor and the Parish Medical Officer as well as being answerable to a certain extent to the General Board of Lunacy's Visiting Commissioners. The amount payable to guardians was fixed by Parish Councils and intimated to the General Board and some attempt was made to check standards of care and value for money.

It is clear that boarding-out was a direct forerunner of guardianship but as such it contained the ambiguities of care and control purposes. Care in that it was recognised that mentally unsound persons should not be allowed to wander untended, control in that they should not be free to be "dangerous and annoying" but that also the provisions should reflect minimum financial call on locally provided resources.

Reports: General Board of Commissioners in Lunacy for Scotland, General Board of Control, Mental Welfare Commission

From the first Annual Report of 1859 through to present times the General Board of Commissioners in Lunacy, succeeded by the General Board of Control and the Mental Welfare Commission have recorded the statistics and situations of mentally disordered persons managed under the boarding-out system and/or guardianship.

The Commissions had to distinguish among the following categories:

1. Non-Paupers

    (a) Living with relatives.

    (b) Living with persons not related to them

2. Paupers
    (a) Living with relatives.

    (b) Living with persons not related to them.

The Board of Lunacy had only "limited control"[12] in relation to the non-pauper insane in that they visited at stated intervals when persons were boarded-out with strangers under a Sheriff's Warrant. Although the requirement of law was that such placements should be under a Sheriff's Order, it was in the words of Dr Mitchell

"So extensively evaded as to be practically a dead letter".

He went on to say

"This is greatly to be regretted, as the enquiries of the Commissioners leave no doubt as to the existence of abuses, which in consequence of this evasion, it is not in their power to correct".

The inference was that there was no public will to enforce the Statutory Inspection as the "private" control was being exercised at no cost to parochial funds. Non-paupers living with relatives were subject to even less control by the Lunacy Board.

"...there being very properly an unwillingness to interfere while the patients are under the care of their natural guardians, and are supported without parochial or other public assistance".

Although the Board of Lunacy could not intervene unless called into a situation, they claimed that in compliance with the 1857 Act, they had to examine all classes in whatever circumstances to report on "the extent and condition of mental disease in the country". 2,508 visits were made and a further 1,504 reports submitted. Of the non-pauper class "4.6% were in affluent circumstances, 25.3% in comfortable and 70.1% in straitened or indigent circumstances". The Board were much concerned by the latter group, not just because they might be living in poor conditions, but because they fed the roll of pauper lunatics - when eventually reported to the Board for confirmation as a pauper lunatic, it was usual that the pauperism was new but the lunacy was chronic and of long duration.

In contrast, however, pauper lunatics in private dwellings were under the direct supervision of the Board and it was this group - 33% of all insane persons in Scotland in 1862 - which was regarded as the success story of the

Board's supervisory functions and the boarding-out system. In Dr Mitchell's commentary of 1864, the word guardianship is used in reference to these procedures;

> "....The Board had insisted on the appointment of an efficient guardian to save the patient from destruction by fire",

> "...A visit was paid to an aged and frail woman, who believes herself to be Queen of the universe, who speaks in unknown tongues, and who had at the time of the visit, 7 dogs, 8 cats and 12 hens in a small room,.... It is said that she persists in living alone and will not submit to guardianship".

The Reports of ensuing years regularly commented on the advantages of guardianship/boarding-out and various different aspects were given mention. The Report of 1878 describes the opportunity given by the system as being

> "to avoid removing him (pauper lunatic) from all participation in scenes of ordinary life"

and claims for those subject to guardianship in private dwellings

> "lower mortality rates, circumstances not adverse to health and the sense of freedom".

This Report also describes Government Grants now being available to aid local expenditure on lunatics and a certificate from the Board being required to the effect that the lunatic was being satisfactorily provided for before the claim could be made. The comment was made that the certificate could be withheld until improvements in conditions were made and the Board expressed the view that the monetary advantage was likely to be effective in achieving the Board's ends.

In the 1893 Report, Dr Fraser, Commissioner, described having visited 1,000 boarded-out patients in the year and inter alia said

> "On reviewing the private dwelling system as a whole, my opinion is that there is no harmful influence on the guardian from the presence of the insane in their houses and this is the verdict of a host of guardians to whom I have spoken on the subject".

History of Guardianship

In the 1903 Report, Medical Commissioner, Dr Sutherland commented in positive terms about the bonds of attachment between guardians and patients and to the latters' longevity. In 1908 the Board's fiftieth Annual Report revealed continuing concern for the private patients in dwellings not coming under the responsibility of the Board and the gaps in knowledge about these patients. In the same Report, Dr McPherson, another Commissioner, illustrated one of the standards used in judging the acceptability of the placement in writing about the level of care and comfort accorded to some patients in rural areas,

> "In no single instance however did the welfare or comfort of patients appear inferior to that of their guardians".

Dr McPherson stressed the importance of seeing that patients were not kept apart from the family or in any way treated as persons not sharing fully in the common household life. He had warned a guardian who was licensed to have 4 patients that he would move those of the 4 who did not have a seat at the family table.

The General Board of Control

The Mental Deficiency and Lunacy (Scotland) Act of 1913 brought into being a General Board of Control which took over the work of the Lunacy Commission. Mid controversy, it put mentally defective people into the same range of legislation as mentally ill people. Of lesser general significance but important for our purpose, it formalised guardianship in that it endorsed the need for a Sheriff's Order with the sanction of the General Board of Control and gave overall care of cases to local authorities. Kathleen Jones in her "History of the Mental Health Services"[13] claims that the concept of guardianship had its origin in the Mental Deficiency Acts. (Scottish and English of 1913). The evidence however points to it operating in an organised way in Scotland from at least 30 years earlier.

The General Board of Control Reports spanning the years 1913 to 1961 (with a wartime gap between 1938 and 1954) record the view that boarding-out/ guardianship was a successful way of dealing with mentally disordered persons, judged fit to live in the community with supervision. Dr Kate Fraser, Deputy Commissioner of the Board writing in 1934 sums up as follows,

Guardianship

"Since I took up duty over 20 years ago, the boarding-out system has undergone gradual but very material changes. There have been changes in administration, changes in the type of patient, changes in the outlook and type of guardian, changes in the work of a Deputy Commissioner".

The changes she described include:

1. Inspector of Poor: Dr Fraser revealed an ambivalence for administration changes brought about by the recent Local Government Act. On the one hand she had this to say

"I mourn the passing of the old Inspector of Poor who, although often a part-time man perhaps not well versed in technicalities, had almost invariably a shrewd understanding and an intimate knowledge of local conditions. He knew the people who would make good guardians, who would treat their patients well, even although in some instances the standard of tidiness might not come up to that of a hospital ward.... I rarely found an Inspector of Poor to fail in his duty when the necessity was pointed out to him. ...The guardian never hesitated to consult the Inspector about any difficulties and to do so without delay."

She continued by saying that some of the old Inspectors of Poor had been retained as new District Inspectors thus in her view continuing some of the good features of the old system. On the other hand she welcomed the administrative changes that were resulting in better and more uniform allowances being paid and better quality of clothing being available.

2. Local Medical Officers: Dr Fraser welcomed the fact that the newly created larger areas would still employ a Local Medical Officer to pay the statutory visits to boarded-out persons. She said

"I have always found that the Local Medical Officer does more than his statutory duties. He gives devoted and ungrudging service. He knows the people, he knows the conditions and the manner in which patients are looked after and is friend and father confessor to patient and guardian alike."

3. Licence: Dr Fraser described the new system of discharging a mentally defective person who had been in an Institution for some years on licence for a period of 3 months so that some assessment could be made of his ability to adapt to home life and to check whether the parents or guardians would be able to carry out the supervision required.

4. Changes in the type of case boarded-out:

"When I took up duty in 1914 all the patients were certified under Lunacy Acts, whereas in 1934 the majority are defectives certified under the Mental Deficiency and Lunacy (Scotland) Act. In my district for 1934, 391 patients were certified as lunatics and 654 as mental defectives. During the years under review there has been a steady decrease of lunatics boarded-out and a steady increase of mental defectives."

5. Guardians: Dr Fraser wrote that younger people were taking on the duties of guardianship and that they displayed a keen interest in the welfare and happiness of their charges.

"Naturally the type of guardian has changed considerably during 20 years, particularly with such changing economic conditions and with the changed type of patient to be cared for. The old type of guardian who was so much in evidence in 1914 is rapidly dying out. During the years of the War it was difficult to get new and good guardians and at that time some of the newer guardians were not too satisfactory. That phase has passed and there are now springing up a new and younger set of men and women who are taking on the duties of guardianship."

Dr Fraser went on to report

"It is worthy of remark that when I took 2 of the Commissioners of the English Board of Control to see some of our boarded-out cases, one of the things with which they were most impressed was the intelligence, culture, simplicity and kindheartedness of our guardians".

The Board of Control Reports continued to uphold the efficacy of boarding-out/guardianship and revealed it to be still admired by other countries. Dr Laura Mill, Commissioner, writing in 1938 said

Guardianship

> "During my holiday this year I visited the United States of America. Boarding-out had been practised for a number of years in one or two States, but I was interested to learn that some States which had never previously done so were now considering making arrangements for this method of care and in one I was privileged to discuss the position with those in charge of the arrangements. There are naturally certain differences between the American and the Scottish systems, some of which are due to the lack in America of the tradition of guardianship which is so strong in certain parts of Scotland and which is often a cause of admiration and envy in other countries".

The affirming note on guardian/boarding-out was maintained across the War years although no Board Reports were published during the time. In the Report of 1955 the system was reviewed in the following terms

> "The Scottish system of boarding-out patients in private dwellings has stood the test of almost a century and during these years many tributes have been paid by the Board's visiting officers to the devoted and sympathetic care given to their charges by related and unrelated guardians and also to the kindly and vigilant supervision afforded by Doctors and Local Authority Welfare Officers".

It went on to say that the steady improvement in the social conditions of sections of the population in general meant that the conditions of boarded-out patients had also improved and that the higher standard of material comfort was evident. Reference was also made to full employment, bringing about opportunities of jobs for boarded-out patients and it seemed that a considerable number of such persons were employed, albeit on restricted wages (apparently acceptable to the Board).

By 1959 the Board were referring to the local authority providing "sympathetic and understanding supervision" co-operating with the Board over any unsatisfactory situations which were brought to their attention. In 1960 when the General Board of Control was about to be replaced by the Mental Welfare Commission under the terms of the new Mental Health (Scotland) Act 1960, the Board were still reporting on the high standards of guardianship.

The Royal Commission 1954-1957 and The Dunlop Commission 1957 were set up to review Mental Health Law - the latter to consider Scotland.

Recommendations from these bodies led to the guardianship powers which were to remain in force throughout the period 1959-1984 (England and Wales 1959-1983, Scotland 1960-1984). They had argued successfully that under guardianship, a local authority would exercise wide control equivalent to that of a parent over a child. They won agreement that the local authority should have the capacity to act as guardian when no appropriate person was available, but they failed in their attempt to impose on the local authority the duty to accept the responsibilities of guardianship. They also were unsuccessful in having a short-term, emergency guardianship recommendation enacted.

The Dunlop Committee based their successful bid to retain a form of the General Board of Control in Scotland (in contrast to England and Wales) partly on the valuable record of the Board in relation to guardianship. They also upheld the continuing role of the sheriff in Scottish guardianship procedures.

Importantly the new Acts were to be framed to encompass mental illness and mental handicap under the general term mental disorder. There was to be no distinction between procedures for reception into guardianship of mentally ill and of mentally handicapped persons.

The Mental Welfare Commission Reports - from 1962

The Mental Welfare Commission came into being in 1962 in accordance with the Mental Health (Scotland) Act 1960, succeeding the General Board of Control. Guardianship supervision became one of the clearly stated duties of the newly-created Commission

> "in the exercise of their function as aforesaid it shall be the duty of the Mental Welfare Commission.... to visit regularly and as often as they may think appropriate, patients who are liable to be detained in hospital or who are subject to guardianship...to bring to the attention of any

Board of Management or any local authority the facts of any case in which, in the opinion of the Mental Welfare Commission, it is desirable for the Board of Management or the local authority to exercise any of the functions of the Board or of that authority to secure the welfare of any patient suffering from mental disorder by:

1. preventing his ill treatment;

2. remedying any deficiency in his care or treatment;

3. terminating his improper detention; or

4. preventing or redressing loss or damage to his property."

In April 1968 the Commission published a report covering the period from 1962 to 1965. It commented on guardianship as follows

> "The Commission's duty to visit patients subject to guardianship under the Act is carried out by its Medical Officers".

Many of the patients who were in this category when the Act came into operation were subsequently discharged by the local health authorities and at the end of 1965 the number under statutory guardianship had been reduced to about 1,100 as compared with about 2,600 at 1 June 1962.

These patients had been visited by the Commission's Medical Officers at least once a year... The Medical Officers affirmed that the standard of care and conditions were in general satisfactory. In some instances, however, they felt that conditions were not all that could be desired and difficulty has been experienced in certain of these cases in persuading the local health authority to make changes.

In the Commission's Summary of Work for 1966 it was reported that the total number of persons subject to guardianship had fallen to 973 compared with 1,061 at the end of 1965. 250 of these were in placements with unrelated guardians in private dwellings and these were regarded as a priority often receiving 2 annual visits from the Commission's representatives. Now a distinct note of concern about accommodation was emerging in the Commission's comments;

"accommodation for some patients boarded-out with stranger guardians in country districts is still quite primitive...".

Reference was made to the Commission intervening directly in 2 cases, one where the visiting Medical Officer considered that the patient was being exploited and overworked and secondly where a district nurse reported a guardian striking a patient. In this Summary of 1966, the Commission also recorded their interest in patients who were resident with persons other than relatives but were not subject to guardianship. They sent out a letter to all local health authorities asking for details of such persons.

It is evident from perusal of the Commission's recorded comments during the 1960s, that there was growing concern and dissatisfaction with the level of care being given to a number of persons subject to guardianship and local authority responses. The Commission decided to draw it to public attention and a survey was carried out by Medical Commissioners and Medical Officers during the years 1966 to 1968.

"No Folks of Their Own"

In 1970 the Mental Welfare Commission published the report of the survey entitled "No Folks of Their Own" which was described as being

"a report on one aspect of community care of the mentally handicapped".

It acknowledged the Scottish system of boarding-out as having been in existence for 100 years and defined it as the placing of adult mentally disordered persons with unrelated guardians in private homes. It reminded readers that the responsibility for boarded-out persons rested with local authorities in that it was the responsible local authority who decided who should be boarded-out, who should be guardian and who advised the guardian on systems of payment. Financial allowances were paid by the Ministry of Social Security.

The Commission gave the figure of 250 as the number of persons boarded-out and claimed that the majority were mentally defective rather than mentally ill. This is put in a context of there being an estimated 40,000 mental defectives in Scotland. The Commission's interest in this group of persons was defined in terms of the requirements laid upon them by the Mental Health (Scotland) Act 1960. For the purposes of this Report the Commission distinguished between boarding-out and guardianship as follows:

> "The term boarding-out as used in this Report is synonymous with placing with unrelated guardians whereas placing under guardianship includes the care of a person by his relatives and care by unrelated guardians".

The reasons given for this survey were that variations in standards of care and conditions were being found, that the unsatisfactory conditions in some houses subject to statutory visitation might indicate similar problems in homes not being visited because patients had been placed there informally and that the system by its very nature could be resulting in financial exploitation of patients.

The survey was limited to male persons (153) boarded-out officially with unrelated guardians whose placements were categorised as:

very good (care and conditions)	28
satisfactory	32
fair	52
doubtful	20
unsatisfactory	21
	153

In publishing this Report the Commission were apparently prepared to set a standard by which to judge the care and control being exercised towards mentally disordered persons living with non-related people and to an extent commented on their quality of life. They ventured to differentiate between "good guardians" and "less acceptable guardians".

> "The best guardians report well on the patient and speak about him in a kindly way. They look on him as one of the family, he has his meals with them and he sits with them in the evenings. They are well

disposed and give facilities to interview the patient alone. They willingly show the patient's clothing, accommodation and bedding. Typical remarks by good guardians are: 'I think a lot of Donald', 'Very good, no bad in him', 'Would miss him'."

In contrast however

"less acceptable guardians tend to minimise the assistance the patient gives. They speak about him as though he were different from themselves. He often has his meals alone and sits separately from the family in the evenings. In such a home, the patient may be treated as though he were a hired man. Such guardians often resent the patient being interviewed alone and indeed resent visitation in every respect. Typical remarks by such guardians are: 'What can you expect of a person who is daft?' 'You couldn't sit with him', 'No other person in the area would suffer him'".

The Commission considered patients' comments and complaints, their daily occupations, their accommodation, the financial arrangements, including the patients' pocket money, clothing - "working" and "dress" and the amenities available such as wireless and TV, attendance at local social activities.

As a result of this survey the Commission recommended to the Secretary of State that no mentally disorder person should be placed informally with unrelated persons and that all should come under the protective function of the Commission; that a Residential Assessment Centre should be set up so that the work potential and the value of each patient (their term) could be assessed; that there should be a form of central approval and registration of guardians and guardianship homes; that adequate financial allowances should be paid to patients and that proper systems of supervision of savings should be set up. They finished by saying

"Reasonable standards of material comfort should always be provided. Every patient should be given the opportunity of an annual holiday in order not only that some relaxation may be afforded him but the opportunity may be given for him to speak, free of the influence of his guardian, of his happiness or otherwise, and of the care he is receiving. The position of those patients who have worked for many years and have reached normal retiring age also requires consideration".

Finally the Commission expressed it dissatisfaction with the fact that it had no statutory powers to direct local authorities to take action in cases where the Commission felt the standards of care were unsatisfactory.

"A Duty to Care"

The survey described in "No Folks of Their Own" was published in 1970 but it is necessary to look both backwards and forwards to ascertain what fate befell the Commission's recommendations in that Report. The backward look is to the Minutes of the Mental Welfare Commission during the later 1960s and the forward look is to the record published in 1972 of the Commission's work over the 10 year period from 1962, "A Duty to Care". The Minutes show that the survey brought the situation of persons subject to guardianship into high profile in the Commission's deliberations. Efforts were made to build on the findings by sending lists, ordered in priority, to local health authorities indicating the people the Commission thought should be moved to other guardians. Not all Principal Welfare Officers of local authorities were accepting of the Commission's recommendations and much discussion and persistence was required to promote the standard of care the Commission wanted to set for guardianship cases. Some success however was achieved on the financial aspects of guardianship through the Commission's direct negotiations with the Ministry of Social Security and later the Department of Health and Social Security. The notions of an Assessment Centre and a Central Register of Guardians were kept to the fore in the Commission's liaison with local health authorities, Scottish Home and Health Department, Social Work Services Group and the emerging Social Work Directorates.

The main comments of the Commission on guardianship in "A Duty to Care" (1972) were the dramatic decline in numbers of those on guardianship - 2,442 in 1960 to 608 in 1971 - and the concern that many mentally disordered persons were likely to be living in poor conditions, unprotected by formal guardianship. Reference was made to the attempt to survey these people through the local authorities and Social Work Departments but this failing because of being able to trace only less than 100. In the Report's conclusions it was stated

"The position of the mentally disordered in the community gives rise to concern. By 1973 there will probably be some 2,000 fewer patients under formal guardianship than there were in 1960. On the information available to the Mental Welfare Commission only a proportion of these can now be traced. Thus there may exist in the community, mentally disordered persons whose whereabouts and living conditions are unknown, and who are not visited or supervised by any authority. The conclusions of the survey published in "No Folks of Their Own" suggests that a significant proportion of these may be living in unacceptable conditions".

"No Place to Go"

The account of the Commission's work from 1972 to 1975 was titled "No Place to Go" - it highlighted the Commission's continuing dissatisfaction with patients living within some communities for which local authorities were responsible. Reference was made to the Commission's experience being

"that patients are still placed with unsuitable guardians and that officers of certain local authorities are not complying with their statutory duty to visit patients".

In this Report, examples were given of Commissioners accompanied by a senior officer of Social Work Services Group, visiting homes which had been adversely reported on for years without the local authority taking action and this bringing about the removal of the patients concerned, with happier outcomes. In the conclusions of the Report the Commission pointed to

"the necessity for the interests of mentally disordered patients living in the community to be effectively supervised, especially when living with families to whom they are not related"

and indicated that more precise legislation was necessary

"to protect the welfare, rights and interests of mentally disordered persons living in the community".

Guardianship

"Does the Patient Come First?"

The final Report in this series spanned the years 1975 to 1980 and its comment on guardianship repeated the concerns of previous years. The tone however is slightly wearied as though reflecting a disenchantment with their lack of impact on guardianship,

> "In bad homes visits made little difference. The Mental Welfare Commission might press for removal but, having no authority to impose it, often receives little co-operation".

It did however repeat its view of a required standard

> "If patients are placed with strangers in private houses many safeguards are required. These include preliminary assessment of the patient; a valuation of prospective guardians; an unequivocal instruction to guardians as to their duties and responsibilities; careful and frequent supervision of the living conditions; appropriate financial arrangements for the patient; regular reassessment of the patient; an authority to the Mental Welfare Commission to order removal of any patient from unsuitable guardians".

Publication of this Report took place in 1981 and inevitably the Mental Welfare Commission was caught up in the movement towards amending the 1960 Act. In a chapter headed "Changes in the Act" the itemised major points requiring consideration included

> "As mentioned earlier formal guardianship had diminished over the years. This means that there are many mentally handicapped persons in the community whose supervision and living conditions are subject to no form of statutory oversight and inspection. In most cases they are well cared for but some may be exposed to the risk of exploitation and neglect. As the Commission has pointed out on numerous occasions, it is those who are placed in the homes of persons to whom they are not related who may be at risk. Any review of the Mental Health (Scotland) Act 1960 should, in the opinion of the Commission, make statutory provision for visitation of such persons and for protection of their interests as in the case of those who are still under guardianship".

Comment

What emerges from scrutiny of the Mental Welfare Commission's records on the subject of guardianship over the years 1962 to 1980 is that the Commission fought robustly to improve the conditions of persons subject to guardianship by calling for higher standards of supervision and adherence to statutory duties by local authorities, by recommending changes in legislation and procedures and by suggesting the setting up of systems which would enhance practice. Commissioners failed in their bid to introduce Residential Assessment Centres and the Central Register of Guardians; moreover they were to an extent defeated by local authorities apparently not prioritising work with community-based mentally disordered persons in the first decade of the new Social Work Departments. Perhaps one reply from a local authority taken to task by the Commission sums it up -

> "I would point out that social workers.... have many statutory duties including Mental Health Regulations but because of the pressures of extremely high case loads are unable to carry out these obligations much to their regret... So far as assurances for the future are concerned, I regret that I cannot give any....".

It is undoubtedly true however that the Commission's systematic visiting and the maintained contact and involvement with persons subject to guardianship throughout Scotland for many years were experienced as positive forces by many individuals and households. Also it seems likely that, somewhat paradoxically, the Commission contributed to the reduction in guardianship numbers by its work with Government departments to rationalise a system of payment to mentally disordered persons irrespective of their status in households. No longer was boarding-out or guardianship a prerequisite to payment being made to carers.

The Review of the Mental Health Acts, 1959 and 1960

In the first official review of mental health legislation, the Government's White Paper of 1976, guardianship was considered on a single page. Basically attention was drawn to the low usage and suggestions and comments were encouraged.

Guardianship

This provoked a response and the next White Paper of 1978 contained a reasonable discussion of guardianship, largely based on submissions from MIND, The Royal College of Psychiatrists, The Butler Committee and the British Association of Social Workers. The first 3 mentioned suggested that more use could be made of guardianship and that it could be a useful alternative to detention in hospital. Also compulsory supervision in the community or aftercare might result in earlier discharges from hospital. BASW put forward a proposal for a new type of Community Care Order and argued that admission of people to psychiatric hospitals should be regarded as a last resort. The new order should exist alongside existing guardianship powers and local social service authorities should have statutory responsibility for the care and control of mentally disordered persons made subject to any compulsory measures in the community. They advocated that the scheme should be operated by specially selected and appropriately trained social workers. The White Paper suggested that the common thread running through these proposals was that the care and treatment of mentally disordered persons might be improved if compulsory powers did not begin and end at the hospital door[14]. In a reflective discussion, various issues were addressed - the unnecessary detention of persons in hospital due to lack of community alternatives, the dangers of extending compulsory measures to a wider range of people without absolute necessity and the core problem of there being no satisfactory sanctions in the event of the patient's failure to comply with requirements.

The Government recognised that powers of compulsion were needed for a small minority of people but was undecided what they should be and invited further comment. The options they identified were:

1. Guardianship in a revised form - to retain existing guardianship powers, but to define them more clearly, to remove the present age limits and reduce the period of guardianship in line with those for hospital orders.

2. Community Care Orders - to introduce Community Care Orders parallelling Compulsory Hospital Orders.

3. Essential Powers Approach - to introduce new and more limited specific powers.

The government suggested that possible alternatives were a combination of 1. and 2. and a combination of 1. and 3. They also raised the further matters of a short-term form of guardianship, as recommended by the Royal Commission of 1957 but at that time rejected; and the need that some vulnerable persons might have of additional protection and advocacy... "to enable the guardian to consent or to refuse treatment, arrange admission to hospital etc". They also invited views on whether the powers to impose treatment without consent should apply if an essential powers approach was introduced.

By 1981, when the Government published "Reform of Mental Health Legislation" the issues had reverted to being disappointingly simplistic again . Gone were the notions of guardianship as an alternative to compulsory detention in hospital, no mention of the complex issues of advocacy and protection raised in 1978 Paper, no reference to the need for a short-term power and a complete side-stepping of guardianship's relatedness to the central matter of what happens when a person in the community declines to take medication. The Paper did stress the significance of changing the ground from "in the interests of the patient" to "in the interest of the welfare of the patient". Finally the Paper brought guardianship into line with hospital detention procedures in respect of timescales and age limits.

The Mental Health (Scotland) Act 1984

In the 1984 Act guardianship was enacted as:

"(a) power to require the patient to reside at a place specified by the authority or person named as guardian;

(b) power to require the patient to attend at places and times so specified for the purpose of medical treatment, occupation, education or training;

(c) power to require access to the patient to be given, at any place where the patient is residing, to any medical practitioner, mental health officer or other person so specified."

Scrutiny of Hansard prior to the 1983 and 1984 Acts shows that there was some hope in the minds of the legislators that guardianship could be used as an alternative to compulsory detention in hospital and that the more restricted powers of the guardian would lead local authorities to make more use of it.

In fact from 1984 the numbers of people on guardianship in Scotland have remained small compared with the numbers of previous years. At the end of 1984 there were 84 persons subject to guardianship compared with 608 in 1971.[15] The figures between the years 1985 to 1991 were never in excess of 71 but it should be noted that there has been an upward swing from 45 in 1989 to 65 in 1990 and 71 in 1991. (See Guardianship Statistics on Page 102). The 1988 Mental Welfare Commission Report shows that 3 of the 12 Scottish Regions had no guardianship cases at all and 5 had only one or 2 cases; the 1991 Report will show 4 Regions without any guardianship cases.

In the Stirling University based study on Mental Health Officer work in Scotland (1991), guardianship constituted only 2% of all the actions monitored.

In England and Wales the situation seems similar. In the major study of the operation of the Mental Health Act 1983 in 42 Social Service Departments in England and Wales, the Social Services Research Group showed 63 incidents of guardianship, representing less than 1% of all incidents of detention under the Act recorded.[16]

It is clear therefore that, since the Mental Health Acts of 1983 and 1984, guardianship has not been used extensively.

Summing up the Historical Background

From what is a fairly complex background, it can be seen that mentally disordered persons (and of course the terminology has altered over the years) have always been subject to varying degrees of organised care and control. The juxtaposition of these two factors has survived changes in law, attitudes and practice to this day and will be seen to continue to be pertinent in the contemporary debate. Guardianship in its various forms has been used regularly to provide a level of protection and a measure of control. All manner of variables are there in the past in relation to individuals but it is clear that the financial status of the person concerned was central to the way in which his/her management was arranged. We simply do not know what fate befell many in private circumstances and what balance was struck between care and control. As long as there were no calls on public funds there appeared to be little will to examine what was happening to mentally disordered persons living with their families or with strangers for profit although some concern for the latter group emerges as a theme across the years.

Historically there was little differentiation between mentally ill and mentally handicapped persons for the purposes of guardianship until the 1913 Mental Deficiency Acts. From then on it appears that guardianship became more widely used in respect of those with a mental handicap, with a falling off in use amongst those with mental illness culminating in the 1984 position of its rare application to mentally ill persons.

We have seen that most is known about guardianship where public money had to be spent because aspects of both care and control were monitored. It certainly appears that for more than 100 years guardianship, organised within the Scottish boarding-out system, was regarded as a successful way of protecting, managing and being fiscally responsible for mentally disordered persons. Indeed it was the falling-away of use of guardianship and the resultant lack of knowledge about those living in informal situations that brought about the persistent notes of concern which were in evidence from the mid-1960s onwards. Why guardianship should fall into desuetude is not entirely clear but it certainly appears to be linked to changing patterns of payment to those caring for mentally disordered persons and changes within local authority services. On the information available, it seems that decisions were made to terminate or avoid guardianship partly because of changing attitudes towards people with mental disorder but also because of the costs attached to achieving a formalised standard of care.

Guardianship had come to require assessment of the persons for whom it was being proposed, their care needs as well as their control needs, and that was likely to result in calls on resources. It seemed that when no guardianship order was required to command maintenance payments then the control needed was regarded as manageable without formality and apparently without much thought of the individual's rights.

The 1960 Mental Health (Scotland) Act gave the guardian powers of control over the patient which were in effect the wide, general powers of a father over a child of less than 14 years of age. In the late 1970s when the need for amendment to the Act was being debated, the fact that the numbers subject to guardianship had dwindled was explained in terms of the powers being wide, somewhat ill-defined and paternalistic to the extent of being out of keeping with modern attitudes to care of the mentally disordered. (White Paper 1981).

Interesting discussions among mental health practitioners, politicians and legislators led to what some thought was a disappointing decision to adopt an essential power approach to ensure residence, access to helping agencies and attendance for training and occupation. The new purpose of guardianship was to be "in the interests of the welfare" of the patient rather than the previous more diffuse "in the interest" of the patient. Apparently the hope was that a new era of guardianship would be set fair.

This did not prove to be so and guardianship during the second half of the 80s and early 90s continued to be used in respect of only small numbers of people. The reasons for this have become the subject of debate along with the growing opinion that guardianship legislation requires further amendment if it is to make any useful contribution to the care and control of mentally disordered persons with welfare needs.

---

[1] GOSTIN. L. –"The Court of Protection" MIND, London 1983.
[2] McLAUGHLIN, P. – "Guardianship of the Person" (Chap 4) National Institute of Mental Retardation, Ontario 1979.
[3] BATESON, M. – "Borough Customs", Vol. 1, London, Bernard Quaritch 1904.
[4] BATESON, M. – "OP CIT". Quaritch 1904.
[5] The Resport of the Royal Lunacy Commission for Scotland, 1857.
[6] WARD, A D, – "Scots Law and the Mentally Handicapped", Scottish Society for the Mentally Handicapped, 1984.

[7] MACKAY, G A – "Practice of the Scottish Poor Law", Green & Sons, Edinburgh 1907.
[8] McGREGOR, C E – "Mental Health Officers: A Study of Professional Practice", Stirling University 1983.
[9] MACKAY, G A – "Practice of the Scottish Poor Law", Green & Sons, Edinburgh 1907.
[10] MITCHELL, A – "The Insane in Private Dwellings", Edinburgh. Edmonston & Douglas 1864.
[11] SUTHERLAND, J F – "The Insane Poor in Private Dwellings and Licensed Houses", E & S Livingstone 1897. (Reprint).
[12] MITCHELL, A – 1864 OP CIT.
[13] JONES, K – "History of Mental Health Services", Routledge & Keegan Paul, 1972 London.
[14] Review of the Mental Health Act 1959, Cmnd. 7320.
[15] Mental Welfare Commission Reports.
[16] M BARNES, R BOWL, M FISHER 1986 "The Mental Health Act 1983 and Social Services" – Research, Policy and Planning, Vol 4.

CHAPTER 2

Anyone attempting to review the contemporary literature on guardianship is confronted with the fact that there is very little of it. As a subject for writing and research, guardianship has not commanded significant attention particularly across the early years of the 1984 Act. There are, however, some signs of change in that recently written material is emerging with Edinburgh University completing a study titled "Mental Health Officers and Guardianship of the Person" (1989) and with the publication of Adrian Ward's second book "The Power to Act " 1990. The Scottish Law Commission has published Discussion Paper No. 94 on protective arrangements for mentally disabled adults including guardianship, the British Association of Social Workers is preparing a pamphlet on the use of guardianship in England and Wales, Scotland and Northern Ireland, and Social Work Services Group is conducting research on the subject.

The fact that guardianship has had scant "on paper" attention hitherto is probably explained by the concentration of effort having had to be on detention procedures in the immediate aftermath of the new legislation. It has taken time for people to get round to thinking about guardianship in its 1984 terms and longer, apparently, to writing about it. There is also the continuing low incidence of use, resulting in few professionals having direct experience of working with guardianship.

The absence of what can be termed literature, however, should not be taken as indicative of no written-up interest in guardianship. There is a certain amount of valuable comment which is in form of Journal articles and reports of study days, some of it in case example format. Also there is written material, directly pertinent to the circumstances of individuals on guardianship, in Social Work and Mental Welfare Commission records which influences thinking but which is not publicly available. The 6 Annual Reports of the Mental Welfare Commission since 1984 contain regular, even if somewhat limited comment on guardianship.

Consequently, for the purpose of this review, the meagre supply of writing on the subject of guardianship has been taken to justify the inclusion of some English and a little International material, where the substance appears relevant to the Scottish scene.

Guardianship

It can be stated at the outset that what literature there is seems to suggest a general dissatisfaction with guardianship in its present format and it is for this reason that the Scottish Law Commission has it under consideration and that others are debating the issues.

The "Unpopularity" of Guardianship

Two who did write on guardianship in the "immediate" post-1984 period are Adrian Ward in 1984[1] and Philip Bean in 1986[2].

Bean's work makes useful links with the historical perspective outlined in our previous Chapter. He argues that modern legislation in mental health is dependent on earlier legislation and that this is particularly true of guardianship in detail and conception. The functions and powers of those operating the legislation have remained largely unchanged, although older moral directives have been translated into up-to-date structures using modern idioms and language. So, instead of the Poor Law guardians, we have the local authority while the Poor Law Relieving Officer has been replaced by the Approval Social Worker/Mental Health Officer and, as under the 1913 Act, approved practitioners made medical recommendations so it is under the Acts of 1983 and 1984. Bean states that the basic mixture of care and control has been retained as before; there may be new justifications, and even new forms of language, but these serve only to mask the essential sameness. Guardianship remains what it always was; a device to care for patients needing care and to control patients needing control. Those who framed the Poor Law, recognised the importance of these two features, so too apparently did those framing the current Acts, although the control element has tended to be played down.

Bean highlights the dwindling use of guardianship under the 1959 and 1960 Act and the view prevalent in the late 70s and early 80s that the powers of the guardian were excessive, denoting a paternalistic attitude to people with mental disorder. He states that in the Parliamentary debates on the 1983/84 Acts, member after member spoke of guardianship with enthusiasm, perhaps associating it with community care and perhaps seeing it as a less expensive alternative to compulsory hospitalisation. Parliament's solution was to reduce the powers of the guardian and to hope that it would be found more attractive by local authorities if it was on similar lines to a supervision or probation order. Bean contends that all of this was an over-simplification because, in spite of the changes, guardianship in the 80s is no more popular than hitherto. In putting forward reasons for the apparent continuing lack of interest in guardianship, Bean states that the local authority will lay the blame at the door of poor drafting of guardianship legislation leading to ambiguities about practice. It is often said that minor amendment could make all the difference. Bean dismisses this by saying

> "Minor changes will not deal with the main problem, for I am sure that that is financial....guardianship is a costly exercise and has to compete with other service provisions at a time of central government cutbacks. Guardianship costs the local authorities money even though it may save money for the NHS".

He proceeds to say that this attitude in social work management leads to few guardianship applications being processed, social workers getting less and less experience and thus showing less inclination to think of using guardianship - a self-fulfilling exercise.

Adrian Ward, writing just at the time that the 1983 Act became statute, was concerned with what he described as misunderstanding of guardianship. His particular focus was guardianship in relation to mentally handicapped adults (the subjects of most guardianship applications in Scotland). The background of his concern was described in the fallacy of "voluntary arrangements" with people with a mental handicap. He states

> "Many mentally handicapped adults do in practice live under the care and control of parents or other adults, or of institutions, without any specific procedures having been followed. Those who provide care in this way must remember that they have no more powers or rights in relating to the handicapped adult than they would have if the adult was not mentally handicapped".

He argues that so called 'voluntary arrangements' are a dangerous misnomer in that the person whose interests require to be safeguarded may not be capable, either factually or legally of consenting to such an arrangement. That such arrangements may be in the best interests of the mentally handicapped person is incidental to the fact that they have no legal basis and do not justify or permit any interference with the rights of the person to be an independent adult. Ward states that in his views the powers under the 1959 and 1960 Act of a parent with a 'pupil child' were satisfactory and that it was strange that guardianship came to be used less and less in the years up to 1982. His explanation reads -

> "Guardianship was not in practice treated as being the normal way of regularising and legalising the relationship between the mentally handicapped person and the person having care and control. Instead, it seems to have been viewed at least in some quarters as a means of intervention, imposed from the outside to rectify a situation considered to be unsatisfactory".

He sums up by saying that the provisions of the 1983 Act abolished the parent and 'pupil child' relationship and endorsed the interventionist model.

Mr Ward, writing 6 years later in 1990[3], is still concerned about the limitations of guardianship, particularly in the area of personal decision making. He states

> "Since 1984 the statutory guardian has had no general role in the area of personal decision making. A statutory guardian is usually appointed only as a last resort in unsatisfactory situations, when some form of intervention is required".

In the preface of Mr Ward's 1990 book, Mr Peter Millar, Chairman of the Mental Welfare Commission for Scotland comments.

> "We need to ask why guardianship is so little used and how it might be improved or replaced".

He goes on to say that the Mental Welfare Commission, in its 1987 Annual Report said that in principle it was neither for nor against guardianship but that it was only too aware of the reservations expressed about its use and of the criticism made about its limited power.

The reservations and criticisms which are documented arise mainly within articles and conference reports. In 1988 the Scottish Committee of the

British Association of Social Workers published a collection of the papers, delivered at a study day titled "Managing Guardianship". Comments therein indicate ambivalent attitudes towards guardianship on the part of both Social Work managers and practitioners; the need for practice guidance being to some extent thwarted by management not developing policies, the fears about increased workloads if guardianship "mushroomed", doubts about the efficacy of guardianship in its present form and strong statements about the vague terms in which guardianship is enacted.

Barry reporting from Scotland in 1987[4], on her interviews with a number of people working in the field of mental disorder, states

> "Social workers have been wary of guardianship, knowing that if it were to be used as a way of protecting people discharged from hospital, social work departments would be rapidly deluged with applications".

She also makes the point -

> "Many social workers worry that these powers (guardianship powers) are inadequate and fail to protect the patient from being exploited over money or property".

Fisher[5] writing on guardianship in England and Wales under the 1983 Mental Health Act, reflects on the limited powers of guardianship as enacted in the 1983 legislation. He refers to the full debate in the 1978 Review and then the disappointment at the final proposals in the 1981 paper, where the Government seemed to be side-stepping the complexities of the previous discussion on guardianship. He states -

> "The concept of guardianship as protective advocacy had been subject of debate both by those pressing for a more viable form of guardianship for all patients and by those with a special interest in people with mental handicap. The principal argument is that guardianship can protect the erosion of civil rights by taking formal powers in circumstances where "persuasion" of dubious authorities may otherwise be used. It might be argued, for example, that an expectation placed on a person with mental handicap to attend a day centre could exploit the lack of knowledge of that person of her or his rights to refuse; similarly, an elderly person

"taken" to a Part III home might arguably be better placed under the protective powers of guardianship because of the danger that such actions infringe her or his rights;"

He goes on to argue

"thus in its current enactment, guardianship is clearly unsuited to any attempt to make it relevant to the need for protection of large numbers of people."

Various other written views on guardianship reflect criticism and dissatisfaction; McCreadie[6] suggests that the restriction of guardianship powers was a mistake as people are left unprotected; Manning[7], argues that the legislation on guardianship requires clarification.

Gunn[8], puts forward four explanations for the limited use of guardianship, an element of professional inertia in the failure to use it, costly financial implications, the England and Wales Act defining mental handicap in a way which actually excludes the majority of persons with a mental handicap (he argues that the Scottish term of mental disorder allows more potential use) and the success of guardianship being so much dependent upon persuasion undermines its effectiveness. Whyte & Hunter in the recent Edinburgh University Study[9], conclude that the law is not sufficiently flexible to meet the different changing needs of people likely to be admitted to guardianship.

Weatherhead[10] in a 1991 article entitled "Why isn't Guardianship more Popular in Scotland?" answers her question by suggesting that there is doubt among professionals about the criteria for guardianship, that the limited powers may not meet defined need, that it not being a community treatment order inhibits use in relation to chronically psychotic patients, that lack of sanctions limits practical usefulness and that non-named guardians and lack of resources can deter effectiveness.

Benbow & Germany[11] two Consultant Psychiatrists in an article entitled "Guardianship Orders: under-used and under-valued" suggest that guardianship use varies from one social service department to another, some encouraging use others vetoing use. They sum up

"If we regard guardianship orders as potentially valuable, it is iniquitous for them to be available to some people and not to others merely as a consequence of local departmental policies".

In summary guardianship appears to be unpopular for a number of reasons, perceived if not actual.

1. It presents local authorities with financial and resource implications which cannot be met.

2. The powers are so limited that they do not meet the needs of those they should be designed to protect.

3. The terms in which guardianship is enacted, are lacking in clarity and open to misunderstanding.

4. Guardianship is subject to a negative cycle - it is poorly understood, is not used by social workers, does not get shaped up by professional attention and continues to make little positive impact.

5. Some social work departments appear to have policies which do not encourage the use of guardianship.

The Welfare Grounds

As we have seen in the first chapter, the terms of the 1983 and 1984 Acts relating to Guardianship introduced a concept of welfare. Alongside the first ground which established the medical basis for reception into guardianship came a second ground which said that it must be

"necessary in the interests of the welfare of the patient that he should be so received".

This was viewed as an enhancing of the social work role in guardianship as it laid the responsibilities for the welfare recommendation on a mental health officer. The Notes on the Act say[12] "the second ground for reception into guardianship is that it must be necessary in the interests of the welfare of the patient that he should be so received. In giving his recommendation, a mental health officer must be satisfied that, without the supervision of a guardian to ensure care and protection, the patient is, for example, likely to suffer neglect or to be at risk of exploitation. The Act does not attempt to specify the extent to which the patient's welfare must thus be at risk before guardianship may be considered necessary. In each case, it is for the mental health officer in the exercise of his professional judgement to determine whether guardianship is justified in the light of the benefit the patient may be expected to derive from the exercise of the limited supervisory powers of the guardian."

Thus although a welfare ground must be clearly established in any guardianship application, the matter of how that ground is to be established is not enunciated and is subject to only the limited guidance quoted above. The assessment of the at risk factors which might constitute a threat to the individual's welfare is left open to debate, an aspect which has received some attention in the contemporary literature.

The 1988 report[13] on the Edinburgh University study states

"The intention behind this study was an exploratory one, to examine how the 'welfare ground' newly established by the Mental Health (Scotland) Act 1984 was being interpreted in practice and in particular the implications for Mental Health Officers, guardians and those placed on guardianship."

The research undertaken in 1987 examined all 23 cases admitted to guardianship during the period from the inception of the 1984 Act, in one large Scottish Regional Authority and interviewed 10 MHOs and 13 social workers in that connection. Whyte and Hunter, the researchers, acknowledged the complexity of assessing the risks to a patient's welfare that might justify the deprivation of some personal liberty.

"The nature of mental disability makes this a very difficult area of work in which to operate since the concept of incapacity involves complex processes whereby ability to make decisions on one's own behalf may be impaired in one direction and not another. This is seldom a black and white issue of competence or incompetence. The MHO must balance justice against the client's welfare".

The main risk factors identified by the group of MHOs fell into two categories covered by the two grounds of the Act. In all cases risk to the person was considered crucial and a multiplicity of social risk factors were seen to constitute the welfare grounds. Interestingly enough mental state was not advanced in most cases as a major risk factor and the researchers' view was that the MHOs were content to accept the medical recommendations as covering the mental state risks. It did emerge, however, that the MHOs in assessing the at risk factors gathered relevant information from a wide variety of persons in the community who had knowledge of the person under consideration.

Ann Burton writing on the welfare grounds in guardianship[14], in relation to dementia sufferers, addresses the question of risk and states.

> "This is difficult to quantify, particularly if the person concerned lives alone and is refusing services so that much of their behaviour is unobserved. It is particularly difficult to judge that an event might happen, particularly if no such event has occurred. It is therefore extremely difficult to prove a potential for harm."

She goes on to stress the importance of using a case discussion, involving all those concerned with the person, to try to quantify the risk.

In another paper where guardianship is considered in relation to dementia, Dr Alan Jacques[15] addresses "the important welfare decisions" and argues that

> "much of the preparation before considering a guardianship or other order should focus on defining the patient's pre-morbid personality and personal style, her attitudes and wishes, her dependence or independence, her reaction to previous similar decisions, and all the other information which helps to show what her normal way of deciding on this particular issue would have been".

> He also advocates the holding of some form of case conference.

The Scottish Code of Practice does not address the matter of guardianship but the English and Welsh Code[16] laid before Parliament in December 1989 does. In commenting on assessment for guardianship it states -

> "ASWs (MHOs) and registered medical practitioners should consider guardianship as a possible alternative when making decisions about a patient's treatment and welfare. In particular it should be actively considered as an alternative both to admission to hospital and to continuing hospital care."

It also endorses the need for decisions about guardianship to be based on multi professional discussions.

Therefore the comment on the welfare aspects of guardianship, limited as it is, acknowledges that the assessment of **at risk factors,** which might justify intervention in the interests of the welfare of the individual, is a complex matter and there is little specific guidance available. The MHOs in the Edinburgh study saw their dominant role as an independent assessor; they all viewed themselves as providing an assessment although there was some variation in how they interpreted the scope of their role. If it is accepted that the establishment of the welfare grounds is a complex matter and that the role for an MHO is one of assessing the situation (in all its complexity) then the question arises of how confident and well trained MHOs are for this particular task. There appears to be little written evaluation of MHO training courses and certainly no identifiable evidence that the matter of assessing the welfare grounds for guardianship is specifically addressed on training courses. In a 1987 research dissertation on the subject of social workers' perceptions of their MHO training, Scott Telfer[17] in seeking to evaluate MHO courses asked which areas of work under the Mental Health Act, a "trained" group felt least confident about; the highest response rate was some 82 per cent who were not confident about being able to carry out the duties related to guardianship. This of course cannot be disassociated from the low incidence of the use of guardianship which denies practice to many MHOs.

Whyte & Hunter[18] in their conclusions of the Edinburgh study state -

> "While most of the MHOs were very experienced social workers, they had little or no experience of guardianship and their practice skills were not readily matched with the demands of the particular cases they were

allocated..... all were working in a context where the purposes and uses of guardianship were being re-explored. The training needs of MHOs are many. Models of good practice will take time to develop. Skills in communicating with mentally incompetent people are crucial and many social workers have these skills....opportunities to share these skills through apprenticeship experience is necessary".

Thus in summary, the welfare grounds appear to present some problems;

1. The at risk factors which might constitute a threat to welfare are not defined.

2. There is no definition in the Act on the extent of risk necessary for guardianship to be considered essential.

3. The assessment skills required to establish the welfare grounds appear to be rooted in mainstream social work skills rather than specific mental health officer skills, developed as a result of training.

4. What evidence there is, seems to suggest that MHOs do not feel confident in relation to working with guardianship and yet it emerges as an area of work which requires a high degree of social work professional authority.

5. Successful applications for guardianship span a wide range of welfare grounds.

On the positive side it appears that basic social work training has led MHOs, perhaps intuitively, to adopt a model of multi disciplinary consultation and case conferences, in relation to the assessment required for guardianship.

Guardianship and the Elderly

Of 15 new guardianship applications in 1985, 9 were in respect of elderly people (60%). Although the numbers were small the percentage was high and there began to be a worry that use of guardianship as a way of managing people suffering from dementia, might bring about a flood of applications. The Mental Welfare Commission registered its particular concern about the cases where guardianship was being used to compel an elderly person to go into hospital. In its 1984 Report, the Commission stated -

"There has been at least one case and several indications that it is being considered in others, of an elderly person being admitted into guardianship in order to compel admission to hospital.... The Commission doubts that this could be considered to be the operation of guardianship as seen by Parliament during the passage of the legislation. Although within the letter of the law, the spirit of it does not seem to be met and the Commission will monitor this situation."

In the Report of 1985, it stated

"the Commission is aware of new trends in the use of guardianship. Social workers appear now to be considering that guardianship is appropriate in a number of circumstances relating to the elderly mentally ill..... Applications have been made in respect of elderly dementing persons who refuse to give up their homes in order to require hospital assessment before residential care."

Again in 1986 the Commission stated

"As before, guardianship applications were made in respect of elderly dementing persons who had refused to leave their homes but were judged to require hospital assessment before admission to residential care. Some of these persons have remained in hospital for longer than might have been expected for the above purpose of such an assessment. This is a matter of concern which has led the Commission to question the situation of any person who, as a condition of guardianship, is required to reside in hospital for any length of time."

The Commission went on to describe the fact that they had sought views on guardianship from a cross section of bodies in Scotland including regional social work departments and voluntary organisations. Among the main areas of concern reported to the Commission was

"The use of guardianship in relation to confused elderly persons".

It appears that over that period, the Commission was mainly concerned about elderly people on guardianship having to reside in hospitals for any length of time rather than a more general concern about use of guardianship in order to move an elderly person from his or her own home into residential care. A related matter is that hospitalisation under guardianship requires that the patient must consent to treatment.

A report on a study day titled "Dementia: Guardianship", published by Scottish Action on Dementia raised the question

"Should guardianship be used at all for people with dementia?"

and then proceeded to the answer

"Since there are people with dementia at present on guardianship, the Courts must deem it to be legal".

Scottish Action on Dementia go on to declare that the objective of guardianship as applied to someone suffering from dementia should be

"a. To ensure a better quality of life for the client. It is therefore essential that a guardianship order be sought as part of a total plan for the client.

b. To give to those working with the client the power of compulsory action. It was considered that the limited use of physical force would be acceptable.

c. To place the client in a position of experiencing a service which he/she was otherwise declining, but which he/she might come to accept voluntarily. It was not felt that continued compulsory detention could be of benefit to the client."

That guardianship should not be over-ruled as a management strategy for those suffering from dementia, is further underlined in a Guide for Carers issued by Scottish Action on Dementia,[19] where it describes guardianship as

".....a way of helping people who have lost the ability to act in the interests of their own welfare".

Guardianship

It goes on to describe the powers a guardian has but emphasises that guardians do not have a role in relation to the sufferer's money or possessions and that they cannot consent to treatment on the other person's behalf. It describes how the carer may go about the process of a guardianship application. Age Concern's publication "The Law and Vulnerable Elderly People"[20] outlines guardianship procedures and cautiously endorses its use in relation to elderly people with mental illness. It has a number of criticisms of guardianship, however, and actually says about some individual local authorities.

> "many have a rigid policy of not using or not agreeing to guardianship in any circumstances, while others have no clear guidelines or procedures."

It also raises the problem of the client who refuses to comply with guardianship and the lack of sanctions to deal with such cases.

The BASW publication, "Guidelines for Social Workers Working with People with Dementia and their Carers"[21] makes only passing reference to guardianship in the chapter on legislation indicating that it is there to be used in relation to people with dementia.

Thus it appears that those voluntary organisations who represent the interests of the elderly, do not preclude guardianship as a way of working with elderly people.

Some of the written comment on guardianship in relation to the elderly, comes in the form of case material presented to illustrate questionable use of guardianship, successful use and decisions not to use. One case describes an elderly lady who was transferred from a psychiatric ward to a home for the elderly on guardianship as the transfer was against her wishes and she wanted to go to her own home. It raises questions about the provision of resources which might have enabled her to live on in her own home, whether the risks warranted guardianship and "the thorny question of whether someone on guardianship should be given any priority." (in the allocation of residential accommodation).[22]

Another case example describes a successful use of guardianship in relation to an elderly lady suffering from dementia, who when she had been living

living alone had been stripped of all her possessions by local teenagers. Guardianship enabled her to be moved into sheltered accommodation where she settled happily and was able to live on in the community. The point is made that it was important to demonstrate that the limited powers of guardianship could effect some improvement in the person's life.[23]

Alan Craig[24] of Hereford and Worcester Social Services Department conducted a small survey in August 1987, where he looked at the reasons given by approved social workers for not proceeding with a guardianship application. He considered 11 cases where approximately half were in respect of elderly people. Among the reasons given for not proceeding to guardianship application were

1. The local geriatricians saw this power (residential) as a method of removing some of their elderly patients from hospital to a nursing home when they had been unable to persuade the patients and their relatives of the "benefits" of such a move.

2. The consultant psychiatrist asked for guardianship to be used to remove an elderly lady to hospital.

3. An elderly lady was assessed for the need to require her to continue to reside in a rest home. ASW persuaded her to stay.

4. An elderly lady suffering from dementia was receiving poor care from her landlord but died before a decision was made about guardianship.

5. Two elderly sisters both of whom suffer from dementia moved to a rest home and one then tried to return home inappropriately. The other sister persuaded her to stay so guardianship was not needed.

In summary it can be said that guardianship is being used in relation to the management of persons suffering from dementia and in the main the propriety of this is accepted. As the following table will show the numbers are small although they represent a significant percentage of all guardianship applications. There does not seem to have been the "explosion" of applications in respect of dementing persons, that once was feared.

Guardianship

	New Cases	No 65+	%
1987	21	5	24
1988	27	6	22
1989	14	4	28
1990	39	11	28

There are expressed reservations, however, about some aspects of the use of guardianship in relation to elderly people. In particular, applications which result in the person spending significant time in psychiatric hospital. Also the question of whether an elderly person subject to guardianship has a prior right to a place in local authority residential care over a person who is not subject to guardianship, especially if the local authority is the guardian.

A number of the issues which apply to guardianship in general, appear to crystallise around its use in relation to the elderly; the at risk assessment factors, the use of resources, the limits of guardianship powers, the question of whose interests are really being served by guardianship and hospital admissions being facilitated by guardianship.

Guardianship and Offenders

The use of guardianship in relation to those people with a mental disorder who face charges in Courts, is not at all wide-spread. In 1988 the Mental Welfare Commission recorded 4 cases (5%) Comment in literature is commensurately sparse. The Butler Committee[25] (England and Wales) on the Mental Offender (1975) devoted a chapter to considering guardianship and reached the conclusion -

> "The guardianship order is a valuable form of disposal which is at present very little used".

It recognised that guardianship was to some extent in competition with probation as a sentencing option and acknowledged the advantage of probation having the sanction of bringing the offender back to Court. Nevertheless it viewed guardianship as particularly suitable for mentally handicapped offenders who needed help in managing their affairs. It did, however, make no recommendations for change in the law which might encourage greater use of guardianship in relation to offenders. The Thomson Committee[26] which reviewed Criminal Procedure in Scotland also in 1975, made only brief mention of guardianship in saying that in both solemn and summary procedures some people would be better placed on guardianship rather than on a hospital order. This was of course enacted in the Criminal Procedure (Scotland) Act 1975.

Ashworth and Gostin[27] writing on the sentencing process of mentally disordered offenders, suggest that it is unfortunate that guardianship orders are seldom used as they provide a useful alternative to detention in hospital as

> "a means by which the offender can be made subject to some control, supervision and support in the community."

They discuss the comparative merits of a probation order, guardianship order and hospital order and in advising the use of guardianship they state -

> "in a limited number of cases it is possible that neither a probation order nor a psychiatric probation order will be sufficiently wide to provide the necessary assistance for a mentally disordered person to manage in his own home or a hostel, and to ensure that he attends for medical treatment or occupational training and that there is no self neglect. A guardianship order may also be appropriate in cases where the offender refuses to consent to a probation order and some degree of control is required to ensure that he receives treatment, care, rehabilitation, or training in the community. It would be preferable to a hospital order where there is no immediate risk to the public and where it is desirable that therapeutic objectives are met in a less restrictive community setting, and particularly for offenders who are mentally impaired".

Hoggett[28] also makes the point that guardianship could be useful in relation to mentally disordered offenders and further development might come about through the legal profession investigating the idea of its use on behalf of their clients.

The 1990 Report of SACRO[29] on "Mentally Disturbed Offenders" recommends that the guardianship order be retained as part of a range of options for the psychiatric disposal of mentally disturbed cases.

Guardianship

Summary

It is apparent that guardianship is rarely used in relation to offenders but that it does have something to offer when considered and certainly has a part in any review of guardianship.

Practice Issues

A significant amount of the written comment on guardianship, again mainly in Journals, is devoted to practice-related issues and difficulties. These encompass matters such as named or personal guardian, the various social work roles in guardianship procedures, limited sanctions, the parameters of the powers, the relationship between guardianship and the management of clients' finances, the right of a person on guardianship to claim resources.

Named or Personal Guardian

The Notes on the Act indicate that ideally, the guardian should be an identifiable individual, specially chosen, who would live with the person.

> "The welfare of the patient depends so closely upon his relationship with his guardian and the personal influence which the guardian is able to exercise, that care in the choice of the person to undertake this responsibility is of greatest importance..... patients under guardianship will be under this degree of control only because compulsory care and supervision is considered essential in the interests of their own welfare. The guardian's control of the patient must therefore be effective and not merely nominal. For this reason, the patient will normally live with his guardian."

The Notes, however, go on to be slightly contradictory in relation to the statement that the local authority may be named in the application as guardian.

> "Where the local authority is named as guardian, it is suggested that the relevant powers should be exercised by an officer designated by the local authority for that purpose, such as, for example, the Director of Social Work, who would normally delegate responsibility to members of his staff."

Thus although prescriptive in relation to what the private guardian should bring to the process, there is no guidance about how the local authority might be required to personalise the role of guardian.

This has to be viewed in the context of a growing number of guardians being in the name of the local authority and not private persons. At the end of 1987 when there were 57 patients subject to guardianship in Scotland, 72 per cent were in the guardianship of the local authority compared with 28 per cent who had a private guardian. In the Edinburgh University study, only 13 per cent had a private guardian and in the 1988 MWC survey, later described, 16% had a private guardian. The fact that there is a marked tendency for the local authority to be guardian is not in itself a concern but what is, is the suggestion that the person subject to guardianship is likely to get a less personal service from the representative of the local authority to whom guardianship is delegated. The Mental Welfare Commission who monitor all guardianship cases in Scotland appear to have some evidence. In reviewing guardianship in their Annual Report of 1987 the Commission state -

> "one recurring topic of discussion has been the question of who is actually carrying out the function of guardian in cases where local authority is guardian. In contrast to the arrangement whereby an individual is a private guardian, local authority based guardians are not always clearly identified. This appears to negate the potential for a guardian fulfilling a role which is personalised and recognisable to the person subject to guardianship - an aspect of guardianship which the Commission regard as valuable".

In their 1989 Report they state -

> "the history of guardianship shows clearly that its strength lies in the personal responsibility and contact between guardian and ward. The absence of named guardians in the local authority context may create a lack of clarity concerning powers and therapeutic responsibility. Such confusion may well contribute to the not uncommon situation where there has been unintended terminations of guardianship".

In the Edinburgh study they found -

> "only limited emphasis was placed on the personal nature of the guardian's relationship with the client and no specific method of delegation or accountability has been formulated".

They also discuss the issue of conflict of interests in the issue of delegated guardianship authority.

> "If the person actually exercising the power is not the person accountable to the Court, it may weaken the accountability of the guardian and lead to irresolvable conflicts between the demands of the Agency and their responsibility as guardian. Only a Court appointed guardian has the independence of the Court to back him up."

This seems to be a particularly important aspect of delegated guardian responsibility which appears to be highlighted only in the Edinburgh study.

Kindred writing in 1976[30] on the American scene, made the further point that if the guardian is an employee of an Agency, he is subject to a number of conflicting pressures and as social worker may have to choose between protecting his client and protecting his job. McLauchlin[31] writing on Canadian practice, similarly comments on the conflicting pulls experienced by the guardian/social worker who is a public agency employee and in particular highlights the busy worker having to choose between the counter demands of two clients. This point is well illustrated in Scottish contemporary terms by examples of social workers having to prioritise child care over guardianship.

Roles in Guardianship Procedures

The clash of potential social work roles inherent in guardianship appears to cause social workers some thought.

> "The various responsibilities I carried added to the complexity of my involvement and meant I was care worker, applicant (for guardianship), legal advocate and guardian."[32]

A report from a BASW workshop on "Guardian Roles" highlighted the fact that there are 3 social work roles in any guardianship case, social worker to the client, Mental Health Officer and guardian. It showed that there was nothing in the Act which prevented all three roles being vested in the one person - a Mental Health Officer may be applicant, guardian and supervising social worker and reference was made to the fact that this was known to happen. The report also described the various permutations that could take place in terms of 1, 2 or 3 different people carrying out the roles.

The Mental Welfare Commission in its Report of 1989 addressed "The Role of Guardian" in the following terms:-

"The matter of who is guardian when the local authority are successful in applying to the Sheriff for Guardianship has also been noted. The Mental Health Officer in making the application has no necessary long-term association with the client once the welfare grounds have been established. Social workers, officers in charge of residential homes and key workers in Adult Training Centres may be the agent of the local authority in closest contact with the client subject to guardianship, but are often unclear as to whether they are expected to decide which, if any, of the guardianship powers they should apply."

Another slant on roles in guardianship is that in the occasional case, the local authority can be applicant, guardian and landlord if someone has a local authority establishment as their place of residence under guardianship.

Limited Powers and Sanctions

The practice issue to which there is most frequent reference in the literature, is the limits of the powers and the lack of sanctions.

Blackie and Patrick[33] in their guide to the Law on Mental Health in Scotland say

> "one of the major criticisms of the present system of guardianship is that the limited powers given to the guardian mean that he or she is unable to deal effectively on the patient's behalf."

They go on to specifically mention the guardian being unable to consent to patient's treatment nor enforce medicine taking nor deal with patient's property or finances.

In its second biennial report, the Mental Health Act Commission referred to various reservations about guardianship which it had encountered

> "a general feeling that the powers lack effectiveness, in that where there is a power to require a patient to attend for medical treatment, there is no power to require acceptance of the treatment. It is therefore often felt that the power is only effective in cases where the patient is willing to co-operate fully with treatment in which case guardianship may not be appropriate."

> "Another limit on the use of guardianship is that in some cases where it might otherwise be an effective way of managing a patient, it has not been used because of the absence of an expressed power to take and convey the patient to the place at which he or she will be required to reside".

This lack of any power to actually convey a person to a place of required residence is mentioned by a number of social workers writing about guardianship. It is seen as a particular problem in England and Wales because the Mental Health Act of 1983 is specific about the powers to transport patients to hospital under detention orders and the contrast with guardianship orders is therefore more marked.

Craig[34] stating

> "one difficulty is the lack in the Act of any power to actually convey the person to the place of required residence. The equivalent to transport detained patients to hospital is enshrined in Sections 6(i)."

and Manning[35] stating

> "It is currently a matter of dispute whether a guardian has authority to transport a client against their wishes to the place specified"

are examples of comment on this aspect.

Another perceived lack which gets mention is the lack of power to restrain and unfavourable comparisons are made with the powers to restrain in relation to detention. Fisher[36] writing on this says

"...the power to specify residence is much more difficult to enforce with a person living in the community than is the power to retain a compulsory detained patient in hospital. Unless living in supervised accommodation, the subject of guardianship may leave his or her specified place of residence with relative ease: most Social Services Departments would be unable to ensure frequency of visiting which would detect the breach of guardianship rapidly and it may be several weeks before action is taken. Even if living in a hostel, he or she may well find the hostel staff unwilling to risk legal sanction (let alone therapeutic dis-benefits) by trying physically to prevent departure. In comparison, the hospitalised patient will encounter both specific and non-specific barriers to his or her departure."

Manning[37] in 1988 quotes directly from Leeds Social Services Department guidelines on guardianship

"we stress the legal limitations of guardianship. For instance, if a client makes persistent attempts to leave a residential home or hostel, then they are likely to need a more restricted environment than guardianship can provide. Staff in these establishments should not be expected to have to use physical restraint on a regular basis, doors should not be kept locked even if this were legally permitted."

The matter of sanctions again arises in relation to the kind of client who will benefit from being placed under guardianship. Bedi in addressing this in an article in 1985[38], says

"Presumably the co-operative, non problematic client will not be made subject to guardianship...so what remains are the difficult cases: those who are downright unco-operative, those who will not attend a day centre or keep outpatient appointments and those who will not stay put either in a group home, hostel or anywhere else. How can guardianship help them....the question arises as to what sanctions the social worker has against the client's refusal...."

Guardianship

The Mental Welfare Commission in its report of 1987 described the case of a young man on guardianship who ran away from the chosen residential establishment 6 times in a 10 week period and commented

> "after devoting considerable effort to the support of this young man with meagre return, the social work department and to some extent the Commission, are faced with the question of what can be done, within the terms of guardianship, to protect him and enhance his life".

Bingley[39] indicates that the DHSS Legal Department's view is that the policies, unless specifically stated otherwise in the Act, carry no sanctions.

Whilst the above has to be noted, the 1988 MWC Survey showed that the specific problem of absconding from a required place of residence was low (see Table 6). However there will be those who argue that a predilection for absconding would militate against any application for guardianship being made in the first place.

Yet another area of debate is guardianship not permitting compulsory treatment in the community. Gunn comments on this aspect by saying

> "it is possible also that an objective essential precondition for a person to live in the community is that he receives necessary treatment. In that case guardianship is of little value".

The fact that under guardianship people can be compelled to attend for treatment but not actually compelled to take treatment, attracts a significant amount of comment and most views see this as an unhelpful anomaly. Further comment on this aspect is made later.

Both the Mental Welfare Commission and the Mental Health Act Commission comment on the limits of guardianship power. The Mental Welfare Commission in its 1989 report says

> "linked to difficulties associated with the use of guardianship powers is the problem of enforceability. There is no power to convey clients subject to guardianship to the place where they may be required to attend the day centre or a treatment facility. The current debates concerning community

treatment orders raise many similar problems concerned with the practicability of compulsive treatment in community settings."

The Mental Health Act Commission in its report of 1987, refutes the argument that there is such a thing as implied powers, for example that from the power to require residence one can assume that there is a power to take and convey the patient to that place. Their comment is

"....there is a danger in the implied powers doctrine that if one power can be implied others may be as well. If a power to take and convey may be implied for a power to require residence at a specified place, why may not a power to require a patient to accept treatment be implied from the power to require a patient to attend a specified place for the purpose of medical treatment?"

The note of debate on lack of sanctions and the limits of power under guardianship comes up regularly in written material on the subject of guardianship and there seems little doubt that, in the interests of good practice, these issues should be addressed and clarified.

Guardianship and the Management of Clients' Finances

Section 41(3) of the Act states

"Nothing in the provision of sub section (2) of this section or of regulations made thereunder shall confer any power on a guardian in respect of a patient received into his guardianship to intromit with any property of the patient".

It is clear therefore that a guardian has no conferred powers as such to manage the patients finances. This raises the fundamental matter which is exemplified by Craig[40]

"A specific problem in relation to the use of Part III (Part IV in Scotland) accommodation as the place of required residence is that the authority is legally obliged to make a charge for such accommodation. It seems to me to be morally indefensible to insist that a person resides in a place and then insist they pay for it."

Obviously any power which results in required residence has financial consequences on the person concerned. There can follow an uneasy relationship between a person's welfare needs and a guardian's lack of power to enforce spending in a particular way that might serve these needs. What in fact appears to happen is that DSS appointees handle the finances of persons in receipt of state benefits and lawyers or curators manage the person's finances when the amounts involved are substantial. The former arrangements can amount to one employee of a local authority acting as guardian and another employee acting as appointee for the management of the person's money: the latter arrangements are of course legally acceptable. The Mental Welfare Commission in its Report of 1989 states on this subject

> "the protection of a persons property is undoubtedly seen as an aspect of guardianship that is subject to the prohibition in Section 41(3) which prevents a guardian from 'intromitting' with a patients property. Guardianship, therefore, is not an enabling provision which can assist in making decisions about property of an elderly person suffering from dementia or in the management of funds for a mentally handicapped person. For individuals in the community who are not capable of making decisions about property or funds and who are not subject to curator bonis, guardianship offers no assistance. This can be viewed as a weakness in the guardianship provision or simply as a gap in the statutory and civil legislation."

What is written about guardianship in relation to the financial aspects of clients' situations amounts to concerns being expressed about some of the anomalies which arise and about the apparent gap in legal provision to safeguard the property, in the widest sense, of persons subject to guardianship.

Claims on Resources

A fundamental theme in the debate about guardianship is around the matter of resources and whether being subject to guardianship in itself constitutes a claim on services.

The United Nations Declaration on the Rights of Mentally Retarded Persons (1971) recognises the dignity and worth of all human beings and promotes their integration, as far as possible, into all normal life. To this end it declares that a mentally handicapped person is entitled to certain services. Under Article 2 he has

> "a right to proper medical care and physical therapy and to such education, training, rehabilitation and guidance as will enable him to develop his ability and maximum potential."

Under Article 3 he has a right to

> "economic security and a decent standard of living."

Under Article 4 he should live with his own family or a foster family if possible but if institutional care becomes necessary

> "it should be provided in surroundings and other circumstances as close as possible to those of normal life".

Under Article 5 he has a right to

> "a qualified guardian when this is required to protect his personal well-being and interests".

In Article 6 a right to

> "protection from exploitation abuse and degrading treatment."

These admirable objectives, however, lay no legal obligation on the law of any sovereign state.

Gostin[41] writes about the "ideology of entitlement" which translated into guardianship terms amounts to the argument that if Parliament makes a legal provision for a group of people who are vulnerable then the local authorities are in default if they fail to provide the services which allow the law to operate to the advantage of such individuals. This simple statement leads straight into a minefield of complexities such as what constitutes a service, what level of care matches what level of vulnerability, what quality of service, what about equity and fairness to local authority clients not on guardianship and so on. Bean[42] also writes on these aspects raising matters such as the professional determining whether this person or that person qualifies for a service, the contention that sometimes Parliament makes legal provisions and hopes they are never implemented and that basically no one enforces entitlement - it remains largely an ideology. Hoggett[43] contends that English law "cuts a pretty poor figure" in relation to the enforcement of entitlement and has largely abandoned it to the politicians who in turn find it hard to persuade themselves or their constituents that developing community services for the mentally disordered is a priority matter.

Bingley[44] contributes to the debate in suggesting that by dwelling on the paucity of the guardian's powers, an important point may be missed.

> "It could be argued that if guardianship is about providing for the welfare or protection of somebody living in the community, its importance lies in the responsibility on the guardian to provide person power and resources within the legal framework of a guardianship relationship".

This sort of thinking would certainly heighten the concerns around the question of who is chosen to be guardian.

Not surprisingly social workers themselves tend to highlight the practical side of the resources argument in their writing

> "Is there any point in having a power to tell someone he has to live in an aftercare hostel or attend a day centre, if there is no hostel or appropriate day centre place? How long is it going to be before the Secretary of State regulates that guardians have to ensure that appropriate residential and day occupational places are available?"
> (Bedi)[45]

Dooher[46] maintains that new specialised resources would be required for guardianship to be considered routinely as an option to enable acutely mentally ill people to be treated in the community or to be discharged from long-term hospital care with adequate oversight. Others describe the issue in terms of specific cases; does the 85 year old with a dementing illness on guardianship automatically get priority at the residential home allocation meeting; does the young person with mental handicap on guardianship, at risk in his own home, command an emergency hostel bed; does the person on guardianship get allocated to an experienced mental health social worker?

In summary, practice issues emanate primarily from the experience of those working with guardianship and from the life situations of people who are placed on guardianship. Unfortunately written up case material is not regularly available although the forthcoming British Association of Social Work publication will contain vignettes of guardianship cases to illustrate practice. One is an example of practice revealing the gap in provision caused by there being no emergency guardianship procedure.

> "Heather is a 29 year old woman with a moderate degree of mental handicap who has lived at home all her life. Her mother remarried and for 5 years the household consisted of mother, stepfather and Heather. It was noticed at the ATC that Heather was anxious, excitable and acting out of character. The ensuing attention given by the staff resulted in Heather revealing in fairly unambiguous terms that her stepfather had been sexually abusing her. The Procurator Fiscal found insufficient evidence to prosecute but the Sheriff did approve a guardianship application. The proceedings were accompanied by acrimony and at one point mother and stepfather ran away with Heather - another situation where lack of emergency powers left the individual at risk. Once guardianship was approved, Heather agreed to move into a hostel and currently visits from her family have been established and she is doing well."

The Mental Welfare Commission Annual Report 1989 contains some examples which "illustrate both the value and complexities of guardianship..."

> "Paul is a 19 year old young man with a mental handicap. He cannot manage money (although he likes to spend what he has quickly) and is unable to read or write. He lives with his father who is unemployed and who "manages" Paul's income from welfare benefits. Paul made little progress in the Special School system and was offered a place at an Adult Training Centre. His day-time activity was to wander the local town and play fruit machines.

His peer groups include more able, better off and sexually aware young men and Paul's emerging sexual awareness and sense of being constrained at home, resulted in an assault with clear sexual intent on an adult woman neighbour. Paul could express no sense of shame concerning the incident and after appearance at the Sheriff Court was placed on guardianship under the local authority in preference to probation".

"Stephanie is a 21 year old woman subject to guardianship with a mental handicap and speech impediment who lives with her father in a large peripheral housing estate in a city. The domestic environment is poor to the point of being deficient for the adequate care of Stephanie. She is unable to read, write or manage money but can wash and dress herself and is an open warm person, although sometimes withdrawn and moody. Past allegations of sexual abuse by other visiting family members had been a significant welfare ground in seeking guardianship. During the period of guardianship the local authority as guardians introduced home care resources to the household, established a pattern of respite residence at a staffed hostel and maintained the day attendance at an ATC. Further visits by the MWC revealed a very significant improvement in her domestic environment and a strong and happy bond between father and daughter."

"Elizabeth is an elderly lady in her late seventies and until recently was living alone in her own house. She has refused many local authority domiciliary services and was regarded as being 'at risk'. She was suffering an ulceration of her leg and with deteriorating dementia was clearly in need of help. She was admitted to the local psychiatric hospital compulsorily and was detained under Section 18 of the Act. She made a partial recovery such that she was discharged to her own home and under the terms of guardianship on transfer from Section 18. Guardianship was used to gain access to the home for needed services and to require Elizabeth to attend for treatment."

Guardianship and Community Treatment Orders

The interface between guardianship and proposals for community treatment orders has not been debated in Scotland with the same fervour as in England and Wales and therefore is not written up in Scottish terms to any extent.

The judgement of McCullough J. in Regina -V- Hallstrom and Another, ex parte W and Regina -V- Gardner and Another, ex parte L resulted in Section 17 of the Mental Health Act 1983 ceasing to be usable as a long-term community treatment order in England and Wales. Fisher comments

"In the first, R. -V- Hallstrom, it was made clear that it was improper to effect a temporary admission under Section 3 with the goal of almost immediate discharge under Section 17 in order to retain the right to treat the patient compulsorily even though not actually in hospital.... In the second case, R. -V- Gardner it was held to be improper to require a patient on leave under Section 17 to return to the hospital for one night simply in order to ensure that the power to treat was not cancelled by virtue of Section 17(5), under which the patient is no longer liable to be detained if the leave period exceeds 6 months".

Diana Brahams writing in The Lancet in 1986 described this as an "unfortunate lacuna" in the Mental Health Act and the perceived gap in the legislation provoked lively reactions. The Royal College of Psychiatrists sought public discussion of the issue and proposed amendment of the law to allow for compulsory community based treatment. A wide range of bodies such as the Mental Health Act Commission, Patients Associations, National Association of Health Authorities, British Association of Social Workers and others have contributed to discussion of the issue.

The Mental Health Act Commission Third Biennial Report of 1987-89 reported the vigorous debates which had taken place and listed the 5 options they had presented to the Secretary of State for consideration, 3 of which had bearing on guardianship

Option 3, the greater use of existing guardianship powers; 4, the extension of the powers of the guardian to include a specific power to convey the patient on guardianship to hospital where attempts could be made to persuade the patient to accept medical treatment; 5, the creation of an enhanced form of mental health guardianship, where the guardian in particular circumstances would have the power to require the patient to receive medication as prescribed by his/her doctor. Such a power would be accompanied by specific safeguards. They go on to comment that in July 1989 the Parliamentary Secretary for Health indicated that some form of community treatment order was still under consideration and that the debate was likely to continue. They wind up by saying

> "In the past 2 years Commissioners have been paying particular attention to the provision of care in the community for detained patients who are or are thought to be liable to relapse. Commissioners have stressed the importance of active consideration being given to guardianship for this particular group of people..."

In Scotland there has been no case similar to Regina -V- Hallstrom but in one unreported judgement of 1986, Sheriff Younger in considering an appeal against detention under the Mental Health (Scotland) Act 1984 where the person was on leave of absence under Section 27, noted

> "While therefore I have as already indicated found McCullough Js views in Regina -V- Hallstrom etc (supra) both interesting and helpful,......It is important to remember continuously the differing language between the provision in the Mental Health Act 1983 and the Mental Health (Scotland) Act 1984."

Although he did not find in favour of the appellant in this case, Sheriff Younger indicated his view that future appeals might be won in Scotland along the lines of the judgement of Regina -V- Hallstrom. In making further comment in this case Sheriff Younger stated

> "I can see that it is at least arguable that a patient who it is thought may be unable to accept voluntary treatment consistently would be better to be subject to a system of guardianship than to a system of potential detention akin to parole. It might be that use could be made of the guardianship provisions in relation to this patient at a later stage particularly if the approximately weekly injections or drugs proved to be sufficient to control her mental disorder as it is hoped."

In this the Sheriff appeared to be indicating that use of the guardianship powers to require to attend for treatment might be sufficient to ensure some patients continuing to receive regular medication.

Blackie and Patrick appear to endorse that view,

> "One way to encourage a patient to take his or her drugs while living in the community is to use the guardianship procedure. A guardian does not have the power to consent to treatment on the patient's behalf or to force him or her to take drugs, but he or she does have the power to insist that the patient attends for medical treatment and to insist that doctors have access to the patients. Using this procedure the doctors could continue to monitor a patient's case and the patient could remain in the community as long as he or she was willing to continue the relevant drug treatment voluntarily".[47]

There is, however, questioning about the "lumping together" of guardianship and community treatment orders primarily because the scope of the community treatment orders is seen to be about enforced medication taking and the doubts about what sanctions and enforcement can be built into guardianship come to the fore. Fisher[48] states

> "It is the very concept underlying guardianship, that of compulsion outside hospital, which is flawed. Ultimately the use of compulsion cannot be divorced from its institutional base; the compulsorily detained hospital patient cannot be translated into the compulsorily controlled community resident. This failure of guardianship forces us to review our methods of working with people who need care and control in the community but who are unwilling to receive it. Legislative powers cannot in the end substitute for good quality services, staffed by skilled workers..... In the case of guardianship, the efforts of reformers would be better directed towards improving mental health services than a rewording of the law."

In summary, according to comment guardianship has an interface with proposals about community treatment orders but an inevitable yoking of the two is far from definite.

Conclusion

The contemporary literature on guardianship is largely comment on the shortcomings of its terms, the practice questions it raises, where it fits with perceived gaps in the law and the overlap it has with current issues about increased numbers of elderly people suffering from dementia, treatment of mentally disturbed offenders, resources, community treatment orders and community care plans for vulnerable people.

The literature, however, has a validity at different levels, firstly in highlighting issues which arise through using or indeed deciding not to use guardianship as a way of working with vulnerable people, secondly in promoting guardianship as an operational strategy and lastly by indicating shortcomings and gaps in the provision to those who have responsibility and authority to bring about improvement through legislative change.

We turn now to consider the extent to which these aspects of guardianship are illustrated or otherwise in a study of all cases of guardianship undertaken in 1989/90 of 1988 cases.

---

[1] WARD, A D – "Scots Law and the Mentally Handicapped", Scottish Society for the Mentally Handicapped, 1984.
[2] BEAN, P – "Mental Disorder and Legal Control" Cambridge University Press 1986.
[3] WARD, A D – "The Power to Act" Scottish Society for the Mentally Handicapped, 1990.
[4] BARRY, N – "The Great Guardianship Debate" Social Work Today, May 25, 1987.
[5] FISHER, M – "Guardianship under the Mental Health Legislation: A Review" – Journal of Social Welfare Law, 1988, No. 5.
[6] McREADIE, R – "Guardianship, Dementia and the Law" Scottish Action on Dementia Publication, June 1987.
[7] MANNING, M – "Time for Clarification" Social Work today 17.11.88.
[88] GUNN, M J – "Mental Health Act Guardianship: Where Now?" Journal of Social Welfare.
[9] WHYTE, W & HUNTER, S – "Mental Health Officers and Guardianship of the Person" Edinburgh University, 1989.
[10] WEATHERHEAD, A E – "Why Isn't Guardianship More Popular In Scotland?" Psychiatric Bulletin, Volume 15, No 6, June 1991.
[11] BENBOW, S M & GERMANY, E – "'Guardianship Orders' Underused and Undervalued" Care of Elderly, September 1991.
[12] SCOTTISH HOME AND HEALTH DEPARTMENT – "Notes on the Act, Mental Health (Scotland) Act 1984". HMSO 1984.
[13] EDINBURGH UNIVERSITY – Op Cit.
[14] BURTON, A – "Managing Guardianship" Papers published by British Association of Social Workers, 1988.

[15] JACQUES, A "Dementia: Guardianship" Report published by Scottish Action on Dementia, 1987.
[16] CODE OF PRACTICE - Department of Health & The Welsh Office, December 1989.
[17] TELFER, S – "The Responsibilities of Mental Health Officers under MH(S) Act 1984 – Social Workers' Perceptions of their Training and New Roles, in one Scottish Region. 3/1987 University of Dundee, unpublished dissertation.
[18] WHYTE & HUNTER, Op Cit.
[19] "Dementia, Money & Legal Matters – A Guide for Carers" Scottish Action on Dementia, November 1989.
[20] AGE CONCERN. "The Law and Vulnerable Poeple" Age Concern, England 1986.
[21] "Guidelines for Social Workers Working with People with Dementia & Their Carers" British Association of Social Workers 3/88.
[22] LECKIE, T & PROCTER, P "Should Guardianship Orders Be Used To Deal With Cases Of Dementia" Social Work Today 13.08.87.
[23] BURTON, A & DEMSEY, J "Dementia & Guardianship" Social Work Today, 22.09.88.
[24] CRAIG, A "Guardianship Survey", Social Services Research 1988, No. 4.
[25] REPORT OF THE COMMITTEE ON MENTALLY ABNORMAL OFFENDERS. HMSO CMND. 6244.
[26] "Criminal Procedure in Scotland" HMSO CMND 6218.
[27] ASHWORTH, A & GOSTIN, L "Mentally Disordered Offenders and the Sentencing Process", Chapter 7 "Secure Provision 1985." Tavistock Publications, London.
[28] HOGGETT, B, "Mental Health Law" Sweet & Maxwell 1984.
[29] SACRO WORKING PARTY REPORT "Mentally Distrubed Offenders" The Scottish Association for the Care and Resettlement of Offenders, 1990, Edinburgh.
[30] KINDRED, M – "Guardianship and Limitations on Capacity" The Mentally Retarded Citizen and the Law. New York, The Free Press 1976.
[31] McLAUGHLIN, P – "Guardianship of the Person" National Institute on Mental Retardation, Ontario 1979.
[32] PROCTER, P – "Managing Guardianship" BASW 1988.
[33] BLACKIE, J & PATRICK, H "Mental Health – A Guide to the Law in Scotland" – Butterworth, Edinburgh 1990.
[34] CRAIG, A – "Guardianship Survey" Social Services Reserch 1988 No 4.
[35] MANNING, Op Cit.
[36] FISHER, Op Cit.
[37] MANNING, Op Cit.
[38] BEDI, B "Coping with Power" Social Work Today 11.02.85.
[39] BINGLEY, W "Guardianship – An Issue on the Agency" Community Living September/October 1987.
[40] CRAIG, Op Cit.
[41] GOSTIN, L "The Ideology of Entitlement" – "Mental Illness, Changes and Trends" Edited Bean Wiley & Sons 1983.
[42] BEAN – Op Cit.

[43] HOGGETT – Op Cit.
[44] BINGLEY – Op Cit.
[45] BEDI – Op Cit.
[46] DOOHER, I – "Guardianship under the Mental Health Act 1983, Practice in Leicestershire" British Journal of Social Work 1989(19).
[47] BLACKIE & PATRICK, Op Cit.
[48] FISHER, Op Cit.

CHAPTER 3

Introduction

The survey was undertaken using information held on file at the Commission. This file information contains:

a) guardianship forms which include the medical and welfare grounds submitted to the Sheriff Court

b) additional written reports

c) reports made by medical and social work staff at the Commission

All cases of guardianship are visited by the Commission in pursuance of its statutory responsibilities under Section 3(2)(b) of the Mental Health (Scotland) Act 1984 and unless there are indications to the contrary these visits are undertaken alternately by social workers and doctors.

All new guardianship cases are visited in the first 6 months and in each subsequent period of renewal. Visits include contact with the ward, Mental Health Officers, Responsible Medical Officers, and all relevant caring agencies. The visits are fully documented. All 1988 cases (81) had been visited, and file material was considered adequate for a survey questionnaire to be completed without a further visit. The questionnaire was piloted on 20 cases in order to establish a framework within which further information could be sought.

The structure of the survey was designed to address the following areas of interest:

1. General information: age, sex, episodes of guardianship, duration, location, "named" guardians, co-ordination of care, other measures of control, living group and accommodation.

2. A description of:

    Problems: the characteristics of the population on guardianship

Grounds: the basis on which the Court agreed the application for guardianship

Powers: the active use and application of the statutory powers

Services: the scope, volume and type of services being used

3. Management of funds, Court Hearings, "Appeals" and Complaints.

The survey included the 81 cases of guardianship extant in 1988 and as such is the only 'census' of guardianship cases carried out in Scotland in recent times.

Survey of Guardianship Cases 1988

Section 1: General Information

Who are Guardians?

Guardianship is in the main a local authority Social Work Department function, not only in terms of the role and tasks of Mental Health Officers but also in cases where guardians are appointed by the court. Only 8 of the 81 cases had private non-related persons as guardians and only 5 guardians were relatives, all other cases (68) had local authority guardians.

Any change of direction towards personal guardianship with lay, related or non related guardians, will be a significant shift towards a broader role for carers and relatives as guardians.

Who is subject to Guardianship?: Gender, Marital Status, Age and Ethnicity

In 1988, 59% (48) of those subject to guardianship were male and 41% (33) female. Most were single with 84% having never married, 11 had been married but only 3 remained so. No ethnic minority groups were represented.

The age of those on guardianship (Table 1) shows few young people (15-26 years) on guardianship, 6% of the total. This suggests that guardianship is not commonly linked to 'future needs assessments' and the period following special school attendance. This may be an area for further exploration given the data outlined later on the significant level of educational need.

The older group of adults 25-65 represent 73% of the cases and these are working age adults with likely needs for occupational opportunities. Duration of stay on guardianship is on average 4 years or more for 38% of cases and for those falling in the working age range this is likely to indicate a requirement for day time activities if not employment.

The third group of cases was in the upper age group. One in 5 were over 65 years (20%) with a further concentration of 11 cases (14%) being 75 or over. The overall picture was as follows:-

Guardianship

Table 1   AGE

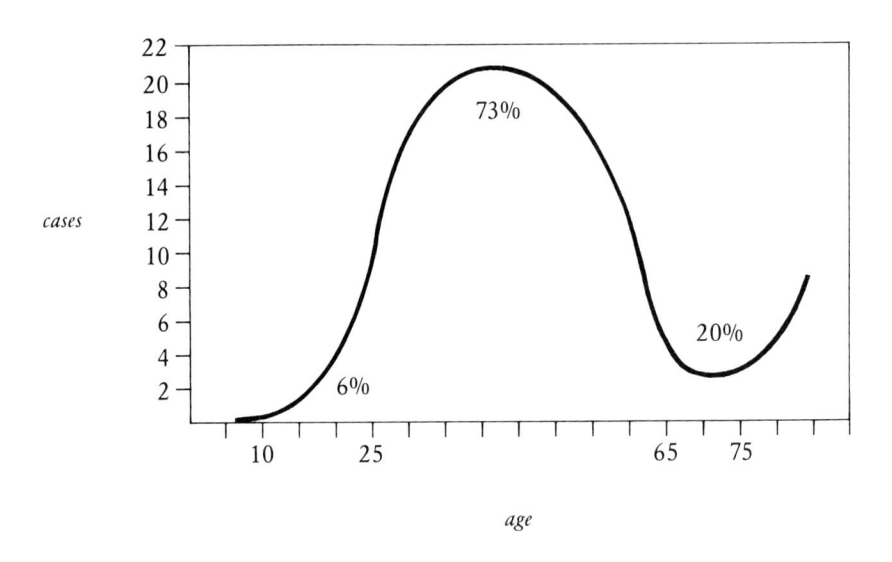

```
        22
        20
        18           73%
        16
        14
cases   12
        10
         8
         6                    20%
         4
         2    6%
           10   25         65  75
                   age
```

Location of guardianship cases

55 cases (68%) lived in urban areas and 32%, one in 3, (26 cases) in rural areas.

The regions of residence were as set out below with no significant number of cross-border placements from the region in which the order was granted.

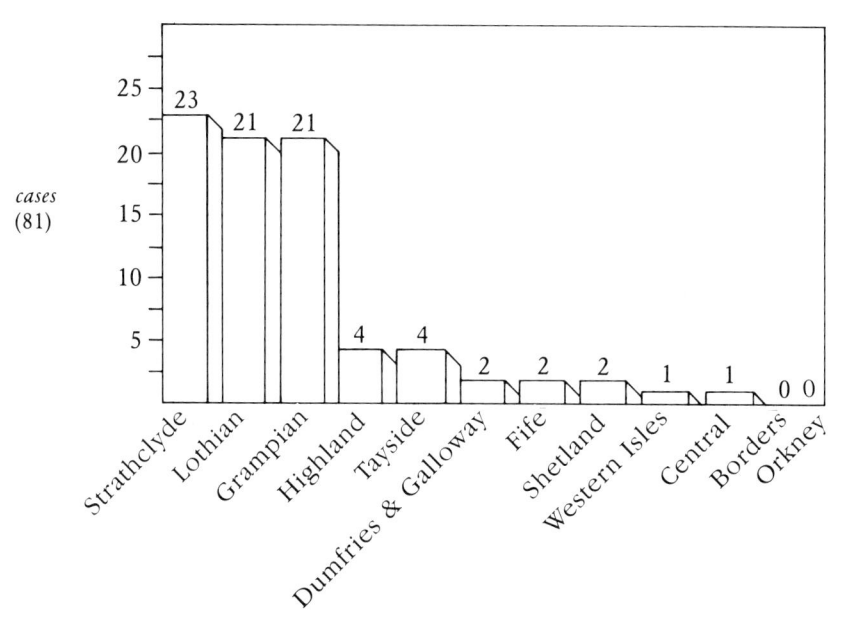

Table 2 LOCATION OF GUARDIANSHIP CASES

cases (81)

Location	Cases
Strathclyde	23
Lothian	21
Grampian	21
Highland	4
Tayside	4
Dumfries & Galloway	2
Fife	2
Shetland	2
Western Isles	1
Central	1
Borders	0
Orkney	0

Local Authority Guardians; 'named' Guardians; the role of Mental Health Officers, Statutory Visiting and Care Management

"Named" Guardians

In 5 cases Mental Health Officers had sufficient contacts with wards to be considered "named" guardians. However, 17 social workers, and 2 other local authority employees could be identified as, in effect fulfilling the responsibilities of guardian on behalf of the local authority.

The difficulties in identifying individuals as guardians is created by the applications for guardianship referring to the local authority as guardian, however, in 23 of the 81 cases (28%) there was a specific worker known to the Commission (and therefore probably to the ward) who had continuing responsibility for these cases, effectively being the guardian.

This kind of contact should be distinguished from the required contact between the local authority and the ward under their duty to visit (Section 43 Mental Health (Scotland) Act 1984).

Care-Management

There were therefore relatively few local authority staff in direct contact with wards as "named" guardians, in the sense that they were exercising the powers of a guardian in addition to pursuing their normal social work tasks.

However a co-ordinating worker of some kind could be identified in 73 cases (90%). In 40 (59%) of those cases it was the person who made the application for guardianship to the court. This would suggest an MHO co-ordinating or administrative role in approximately 50% of the 81 cases.

Non-local authority staff were recorded in co-ordinating roles in 35 cases.

In 49 of cases (60%) other professional workers were also involved ranging across a variety of types of care workers. This suggests that guardianship cases do not lack contact with care workers in general or with MHOs in many cases.

These findings raise questions about the case management as opposed to the administrative role of MHOs. The findings point to the need to be clear as to who is exercising the specific statutory powers given to guardians.

Most of the staff in contact with those on guardianship were local authority staff. There was little contact with community psychiatric nurses; 55 people were in contact with GPs and 43 with psychiatric services but these were not in co-ordinating roles in respect of guardianship. The links with all kinds of staff (147 instances recorded for 81 people) were on average less than 2 people per ward at the time of this survey.

Statutory Visits

It is a matter for further discussion as to whether local authorities can exercise their duty to discharge wards from guardianship (Section 50(4)) unless the visiting social worker can assess the degree to which the welfare grounds are still met. It could be argued that this can only be achieved by regular contact under regulations (Section 43) by Mental Health Officers who are experienced in making such assessments.

The data on visiting shows that in 73% (59) of cases there were regular visits by social workers but that in 16 cases visits were less than 4 per year.

Table 3 COORDINATION AND STAFF CONTACT

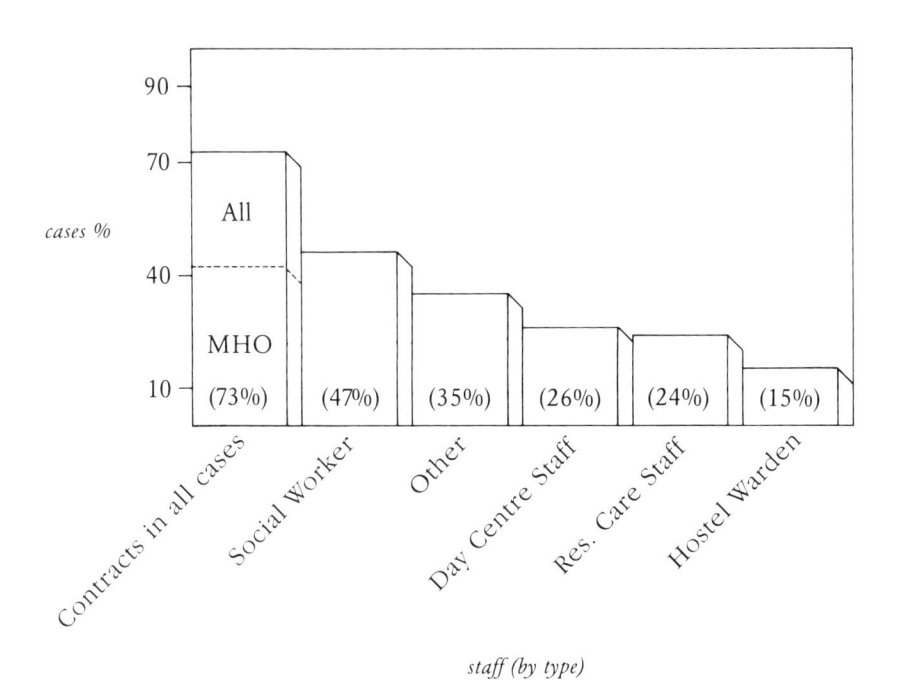

cases %

Contracts in all cases	Social Worker	Other	Day Centre Staff	Res. Care Staff	Hostel Warden
(73%)	(47%)	(35%)	(26%)	(24%)	(15%)

All
MHO

staff (by type)

Whilst the picture of contact with professional staff shows adequate levels of ongoing contact with guardians, MHOs, case co-ordinators or keyworkers, their roles are often far from clear in practice. "Named" personal guardians are rare and whilst care coordinators could be identified in most cases it is not clear that they are guardians exercising powers, as well as coordinating statutory visiting and dealing with renewals. The level of MHO contact would suggest a sound basis upon which to build 'named' guardians who would be competent to undertake statutory visits and make decisions on the application of powers under Section 41 (2)(a)(b)(c) (Powers), under 47 3(a)(b) (Renewals) and also under Section 50(4) (Orders for Discharge) of the Mental Health Act.

Guardianship

Duration of Guardianship

Table 4 shows that 31 (38%) of clients had been on guardianship for 3 years or more in 1988. The residual pre-1984 population was 27 clients (33% of the 1988 group). This suggests that the current activity shows a continuing medium term use of guardianship on the base of a significant number of cases of a longer term nature initiated under the 1960 Mental Health (Scotland) Act.

Duration for less than 2 years in 1988 was reported as 56%. This suggests, although the average duration is 4 years, that there may be a shorter term use, under 2 years (56%) and a medium to long term use for 5 years and upwards (38%). This may represent different client needs and the use of guardianship provisions as intervention in the short term and protection and management in the longer term.

Of the 81 cases 66% (54) were post 1984 and 33% (27) pre 1984 at inception. Given that since 1984 new long-term cases have not been accumulating then it may be the case that there are differing functions which guardianship is thought to perform linked to duration. Nine clients had been on guardianship in 1988 for more than 21 years.

Table 4   DURATION

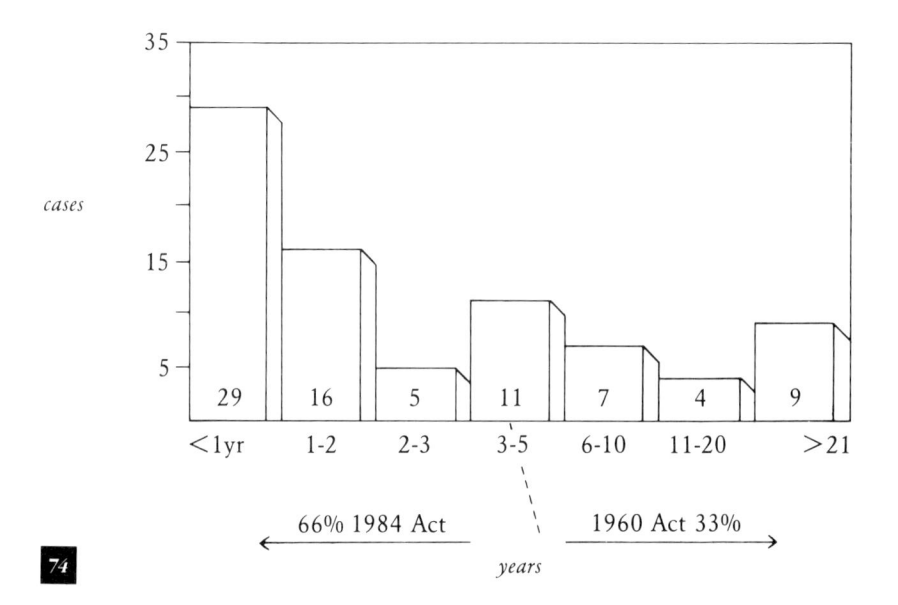

years	<1yr	1-2	2-3	3-5	6-10	11-20	>21
cases	29	16	5	11	7	4	9

66% 1984 Act ← (< 3-5) | 1960 Act 33% →

In considering how often wards are subject to guardianship few of the 1988 cases had had more than one episode of whatever duration. Uninterrupted single periods on guardianship occurred in 69 cases with 11 cases with 2 episodes and one with 3. This suggests that guardianship is not a commonly repeated provision, perhaps because the process of application to the court deters applications after intended or unintended termination of a period of guardianship. It may also reflect a pattern of short single interventions to achieve a specific immediate goal and longer term support built in as an almost permanent form of management and maintenance.

The data on turnover of cases shows that in the 1988 group there was a 32% annual turnover of cases with 26 new cases and 20 cases being terminated. By 1991 there were 31 new cases and 25 people were discharged.

Are people on Guardianship subject to other measures of care or control?

Few guardianship cases, 4 in 1988, had previous involvement with services through the Criminal Procedure Act 1975. However 12 cases (15%) had been subject to previous detention under the Mental Health (Scotland) Act 1984 at some previous time. Six cases (7%) were transferred direct from Section 18 detention to guardianship. A total of 18 cases (22%) were discharged from hospital and placed on guardianship.

Where do people on Guardianship live and with whom?

In the 1988 group 60% lived in some form of institutional care, divided between hostels (23%), residential care (19%) and hospital (19%).

Group homes and supported accommodation catered for few cases 4% and 3% respectively. One in 10 of those on guardianship in 1988 lived on farms.

Only 6 cases were resident in their own homes but 17.5% lived in another person's home. This latter figure is similar to the numbers of non local authority guardians either related or non-related (16%), and suggests that the practice of wards living with a personal guardian still continues but to no great extent. Coupled with the information on non-local authority guardians there remains a basis, albeit small, on which lay personal guardianship with or without residence might be developed.

Guardianship

In terms of 'personal space' the high level of institutional care is repeated in the figure of 38% who did not have their own room and shared with others.

The composition of living groups reflect places of residence, 55% (45) lived in a group of residents, 15% (12) lived alone, 10 lived with their own family and 5 with a relative. A further 6 lived with non-related families.

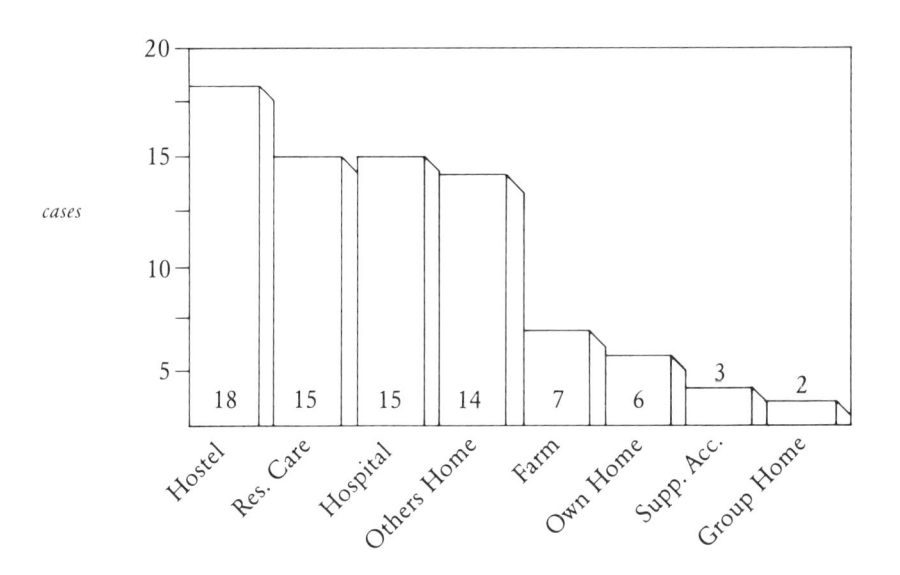

Table 5   PLACE OF RESIDENCE

Place	Cases
Hostel	18
Res. Care	15
Hospital	15
Others Home	14
Farm	7
Own Home	6
Supp. Acc.	3
Group Home	2

Summary of General Characteristics

1. Guardianship is mainly a local authority function not only in applications for guardianship but in the provision of effective guardians.

2. Most people on guardianship were single, few ever married, and there were slightly more men than women in 1988. The age range shows few young adults. Most of these on guardianship were in a potentially economically active age group and likely to require occupational activities. A significant number of people of 65+ (20%) points to the use of guardianship for people suffering from dementia. This survey found 15% of those on guardianship to suffer from dementia.

3. Guardianship cases were concentrated in 3 regions (Strathclyde, Lothian and Grampian) and with a lower than expected use in smaller regions.

4. Few local authority guardians were 'named' but a coordinating worker of some kind could be identified in 90% of cases, in 28% this was a social worker. The coordination of the duties of guardians and contact with careworkers was established in almost all cases.

5. Duration of guardianship was on average 4 years but there are 2 apparent uses - 56% had been on guardianship for less than 2 years and 38 for 5 or more years. Turnover of 20-26 cases per year by termination and new cases linked to the other population of 33 who were on guardianship pre 1984 shows a short and longer term use of guardianship.

6. Few cases had been subject to prior measures of control either through the Criminal Justice system or under the Mental Health Act. A significant number of clients (22%) came onto guardianship direct from hospital care.

7. Most people on guardianship live in institutional rather than domestic settings. Personal, related and unrelated, guardians with wards resident in their homes remains a small but significant pattern of guardianship.

Section 2: Problems Experienced by People Subject to Guardianship

The data on clients' problems was derived from a file search using information gathered in visits to those on guardianship.

Rank Order of Problems

1. Finance

67 of the 81 cases (83%) noted some form of financial problem. 55 people had problems of financial management (68%). An inability to save was reported in 4 cases, a lack of funds in 6, and in 9 cases (11%) the ward was reported as not benefiting from his/her income.

11% of the group were regarded as vulnerable to financial exploitation and a larger group 23% (19) were regarded as "gullible". Sixteen clients were reported as having educational needs in the management of money. No actual disputes over money were recorded. Further data on the management of funds is included in Section 6 below.

2. Family Relationships

67 clients (83%) were recorded as having problems in this area. 19%(15) of the clients had no contact with family and a further 6% had no family - 5 clients had suffered recent bereavement.

Of those in contact with their families 20 experienced conflict with their families and 5 clients were reported as outwith family control. 18 clients were reported as 'at risk' in relation to their families.

Additional problems experienced in families were parental mental illness in 2 cases, other siblings in care in 6 cases, and problems with alcohol in 15 cases.

3. Vulnerability

165 clients (80%) were recorded as being vulnerable, either in terms of financial exploitation (9), general gullibility (19) or being 'at risk' (22).

40 clients (50%) were reported as unable to care for themselves. This latter point links with 2 other problem areas on hygiene and clothing, noted below.

4. Occupational/Recreational

45 clients (60%) recorded problems in this area. 13 people had difficulty engaging with occupational programmes and 7 instances of limited access to programmes was reported. A total of 28% of the 81 clients had some difficulty in getting to or using occupational schemes. 7 reports were made of clients being used as unpaid labour. Recreational pursuits and in particular holidays were reported as problems in 11 cases. These reports of occupational problems should be seen in the light of the use of powers to attend occupational activity (29 cases) and a similar number required to attend training (27 cases).

5. Behavioural Problems

There were 93 instances of behavioural problems recorded for 58 (71%) of the clients. Problems ranged from general anti-social behaviour and non-specific problems through contact with police and reported violence. Significantly, absconding was infrequently reported, and this is against the background of the requirement to reside power being used in 55 cases and a common concern about the apparent or likely difficulty of enforcing this power of guardianship.

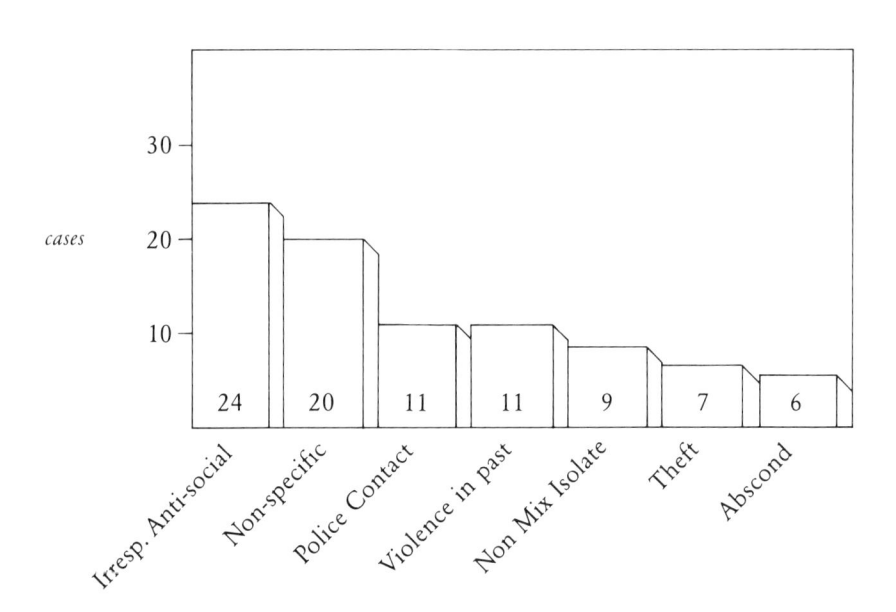

Table 6   REPORTED BEHAVIOURAL PROBLEMS

Irresp. Anti-social	Non-specific	Police Contact	Violence in past	Non Mix Isolate	Theft	Abscond
24	20	11	11	9	7	6

6. Mental Health; Handicap, Illness, Dementia and General Health Problems

All those subject to guardianship are defined as having mental disorder in the meaning of the Mental Health Act. The specific types of disorder were reported as:

Mental Handicap	63	(77%)
Mental Illness	13	(16%)
Dementia	5	(6%)

However, in 7 cases in the first 2 categories dementia was also reported as a feature. This would suggest that dementia is a feature of 14% of the group. This compares with the data on grounds and problems which reported dementia at 15% and 16% respectively.

This problem area of health was rank ordered in final tables by excluding the mental handicap and illness figures since they are a characteristic of the population itself, and in order to assess the significance of other health problems.

These were significant in numbers, 55 clients (68%) had other health problems (including dementia). Excluding dementia however, 13% suffered a form of speech impediment, and this relates to the educational data which records deafness at 9% and to interpersonal problems where communication difficulties were recorded at 13.5%. Significantly speech therapy does not appear specifically in the services received by those on guardianship.

The picture of general health problems shows epilepsy being at 12% and minor levels of incontinence and diabetes.

Table 7   GENERAL HEALTH PROBLEMS

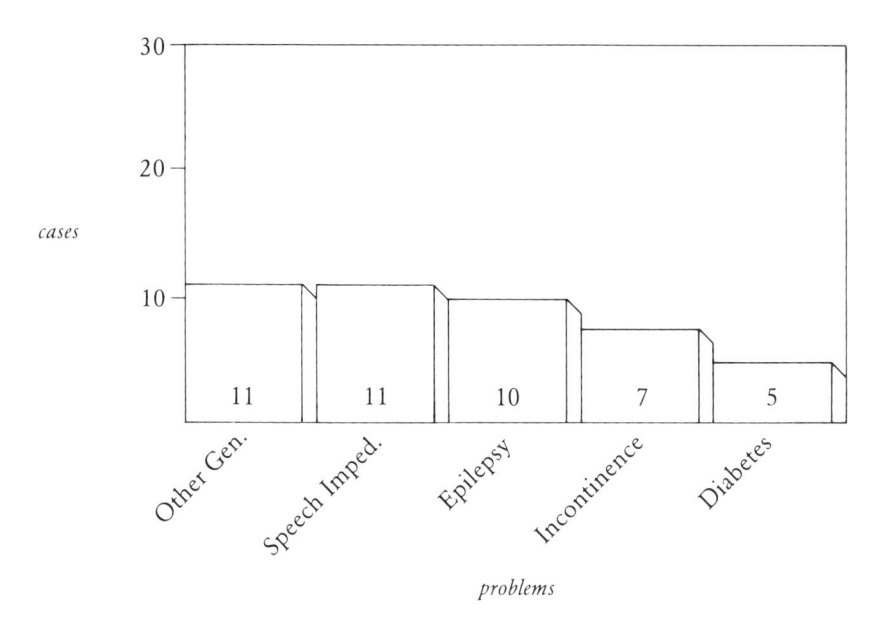

Problem	Cases
Other Gen.	11
Speech Imped.	11
Epilepsy	10
Incontinence	7
Diabetes	5

7. Educational Problems

52 (64%) clients were reported as having educational problems. A core of the group, as we would expect from the levels of mental handicap recorded,

Guardianship

have significant learning difficulties - between 37%, and 41% of the group could not read or write or were not numerate. A further 9% were reported as deaf.

Those subject to guardianship include a significant number of people with special educational needs and these problems can be linked to the data on problems in self-care and hygiene (38%, 12% of clients) and to those regarded as "at risk" (22%). These problems continue to create significant levels of dependency, and inability to live independently.

8 Housing

There were 56 housing problems recorded amongst the 81 cases for 47 (58%) of those on guardianship. The breakdown of housing problems was as follows:

Table 8   HOUSING/ACCOMMODATION PROBLEMS

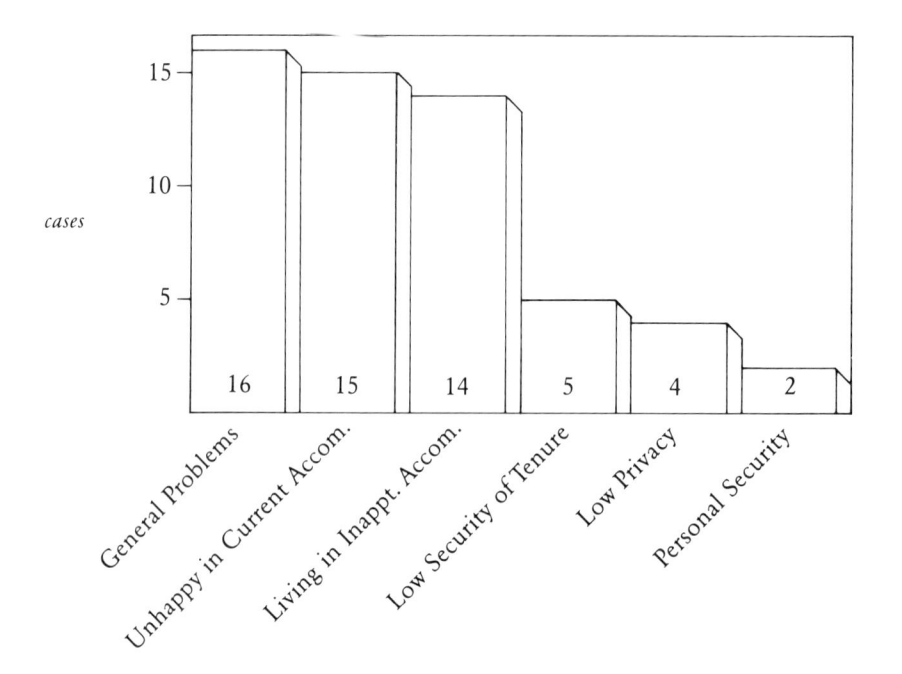

Category	Cases
General Problems	16
Unhappy in Current Accom.	15
Living in Inappt. Accom.	14
Low Security of Tenure	5
Low Privacy	4
Personal Security	2

Given that guardianship provides the power to require residence and that this power is commonly used (in 68% of cases) it is of note that housing and placement problems remain high.

9. Interpersonal and Sexual Problems

These 2 areas were scored separately but are brought together for the purposes of this commentary. 47 clients were reported as having interpersonal problems (58%). These problems concerned, "not getting on with peers" and difficulties of engaging with carer staff, both problems were reported in 13 instances (16%). Communication problems were recorded in 11 cases confirming the educational data. Conflicts with neighbours/local community were reported in 9 cases (11%). The general category of sexual problems was 11% but is shown below in more detail. (Table 10).

18% of the group were recorded as having non-specific interpersonal problems.

Table 9   INTER-PERSONAL PROBLEMS

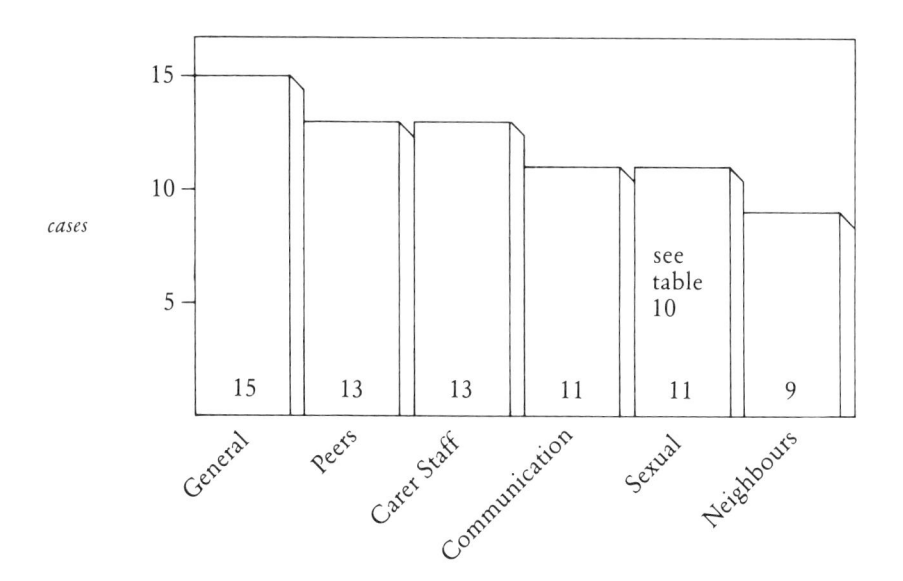

General	Peers	Carer Staff	Communication	Sexual	Neighbours
15	13	13	11	11 (see table 10)	9

Guardianship

The reporting of sexual problems amongst general interpersonal problems was 11%. However to specific questions on sexual problems there was an increase in responses to 34 instances concerning 22 (27%) of clients.

Sexual problems are of 2 distinct types, actual inappropriate behaviour and vulnerability to exploitation.

Table 10   SEXUAL PROBLEMS

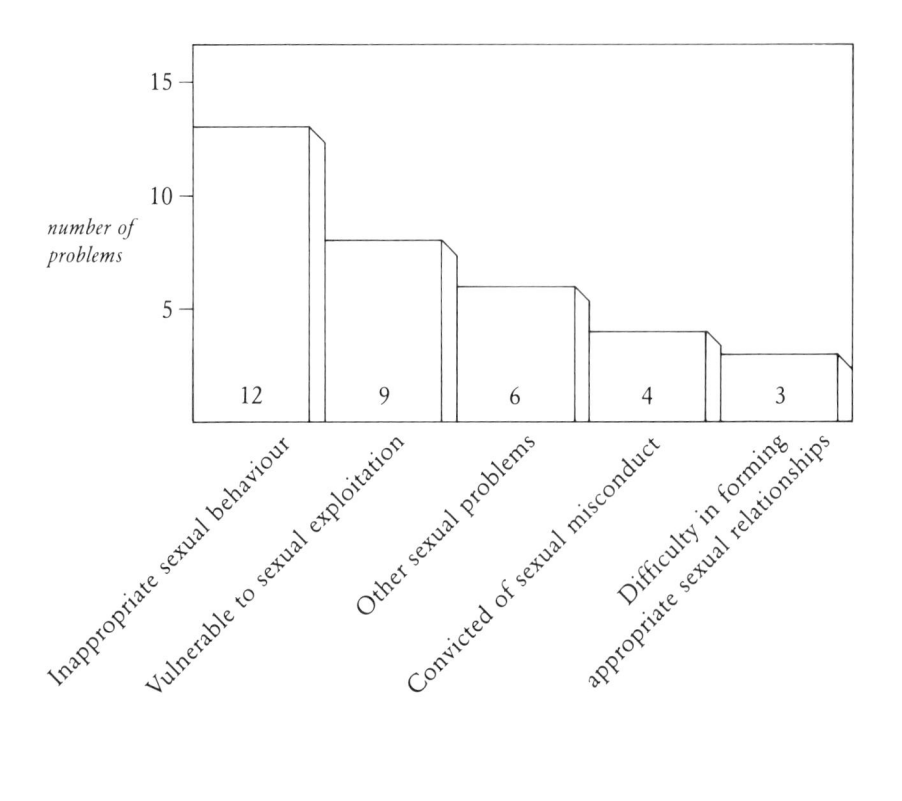

Category	Number
Inappropriate sexual behaviour	12
Vulnerable to sexual exploitation	9
Other sexual problems	6
Convicted of sexual misconduct	4
Difficulty in forming appropriate sexual relationships	3

10/11 Hygiene and Clothing Problems

55 clients were reported as having hygiene problems. 12% required assistance and help, a small group of relatively dependent people as distinct from a large number 31(28%) who could care for themselves but who required prompting. 9 clients' personal hygiene was reported as consistently poor.

46% of clients (37) reported some clothing problem. 38% required assistance in maintaining clothing and with self-care in this regard. 4 people were reported as having special clothing needs, 5 reports were made of insufficient clothing.

Summary of Problems reported for people subject to Guardianship

1. The main group of clients on guardianship are those with mental handicap 77%, but mental illness at 16% and dementia at approximately 15% are two further significant but overlapping categories. General health problems were also common.

2. Those on guardianship have multiple and cumulative problems and most have problems of family relationships (83%), general vulnerability (80%) and of financial management (83%).

3. Those on guardianship are relatively dependent with significant educational needs (64%) and problems in self-care, personal hygiene and clothing. 80% of the group were considered vulnerable, gullible or at risk. Half of those studied were unable to care for themselves.

4. Those on guardianship have a range of behavioural problems, interpersonal and sexual problems. The group is not reported as absconding frequently but irresponsible and violent behaviour was reported in a significant number of cases.

5. Housing and accommodation problems, in particular inappropriate placement was recorded in 14 cases, and this is significant in the light of the guardianship power to require residence.

6. Engagement with and use of occupational opportunities showed almost half the group to have problems in this area.

Guardianship even when a relatively short lived provision of care and protection in a client's life occurs against a background of longer term dependency and relatively high need.

Guardianship

Table 11 RANK ORDER OF PROBLEMS

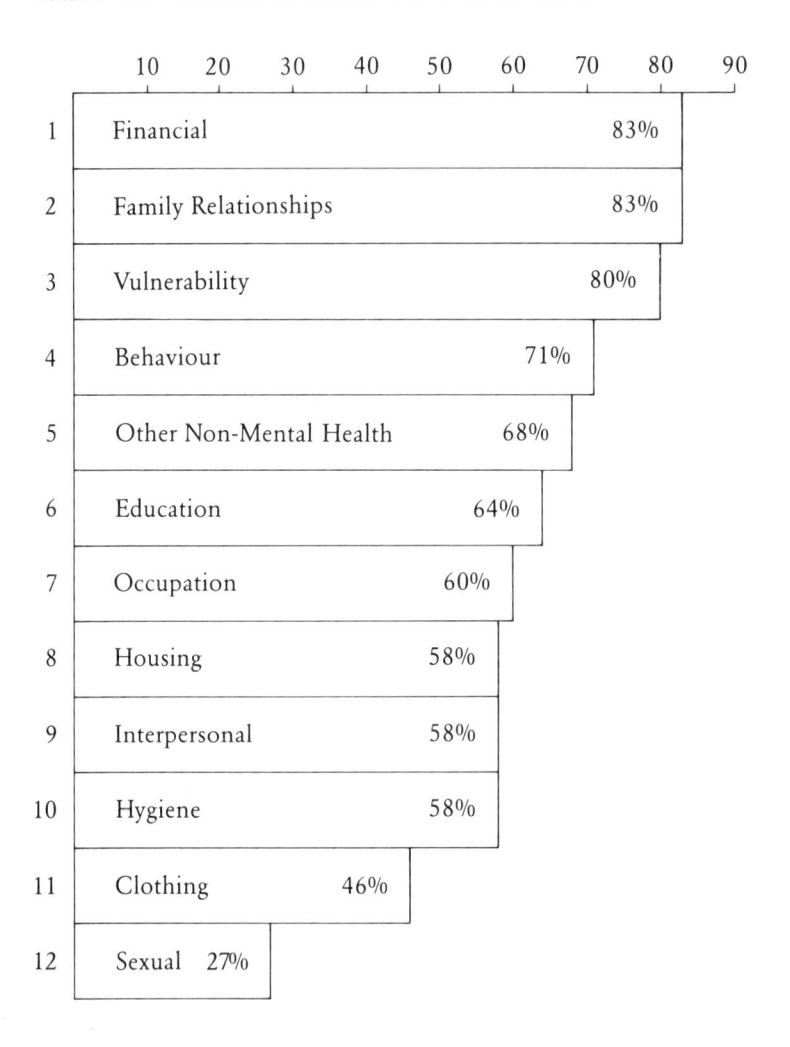

	Problem	%
1	Financial	83%
2	Family Relationships	83%
3	Vulnerability	80%
4	Behaviour	71%
5	Other Non-Mental Health	68%
6	Education	64%
7	Occupation	60%
8	Housing	58%
9	Interpersonal	58%
10	Hygiene	58%
11	Clothing	46%
12	Sexual	27%

Section 3: Grounds Presented to the Court on Application or at Renewal

The survey scanned both medical and welfare grounds for 9 themes ranging from reports on the existence of mental disorder to the degree of vulnerability and the existence of a proposed management plan.

The 1988 group included new cases for which there were 3 grounds, cases where there were both new and renewal grounds, 5 grounds and others where renewal grounds only were reported in 1988, 2 grounds or 4 grounds.

In total, 324 grounds submitted to courts or included in renewals were scrutinised for 81 clients and under the 9 themes, 699 references were identified.

Of the grounds which went to the Sheriff Court, or were the basis of renewals, 210 (65%) medical and 114 (35%) welfare grounds were examined from the forms received statutorily by the Commission.

All types of cases, new and renewals have been analysed together at this stage.

Guardianship

The overall picture is as follows:

Table 12 RANK ORDER OF THEMES REFERRED TO IN THE GROUNDS FOR GUARDIANSHIP AND PERCENTAGE SHARE

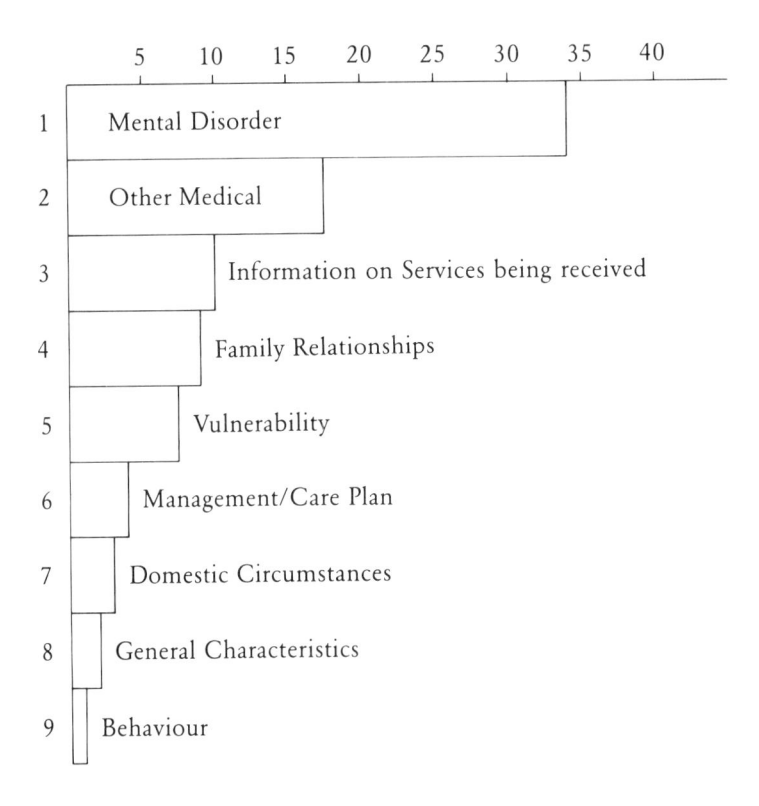

1	Mental Disorder
2	Other Medical
3	Information on Services being received
4	Family Relationships
5	Vulnerability
6	Management/Care Plan
7	Domestic Circumstances
8	General Characteristics
9	Behaviour

Table 13   MEDICAL AND WELFARE GROUNDS: RANK ORDER AND COMPARISON OF THEMES BY SOURCE.

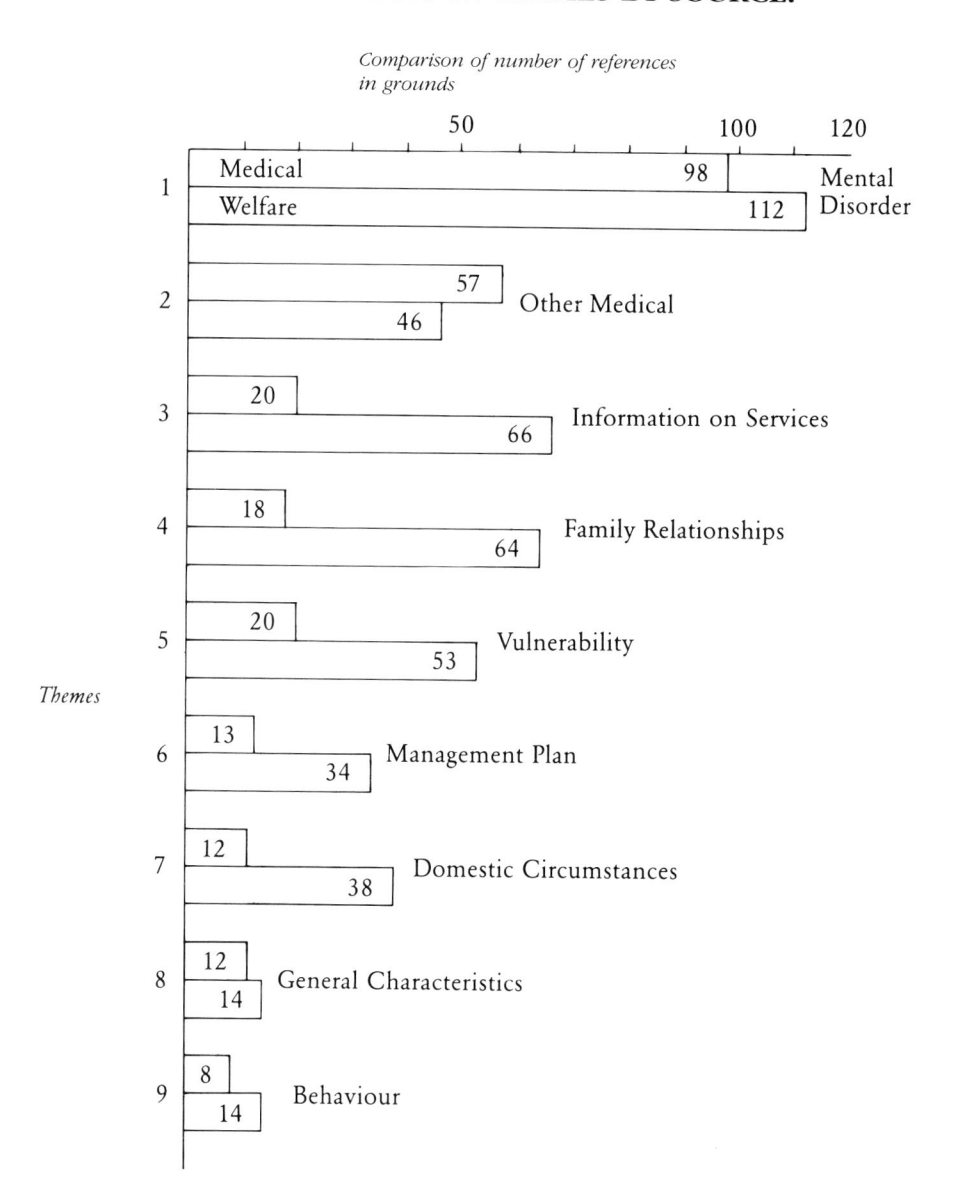

Comparison of number of references in grounds

Rank	Theme	Medical	Welfare
1	Mental Disorder	98	112
2	Other Medical	57	46
3	Information on Services	20	66
4	Family Relationships	18	64
5	Vulnerability	20	53
6	Management Plan	13	34
7	Domestic Circumstances	12	38
8	General Characteristics	12	14
9	Behaviour	8	14

The data suggests that "mental disorder" is only specified in 75% of grounds. Other medical problems are frequently mentioned in grounds. This reflects the data in the problems section which shows non-mental health medical problems in 68% of the 81 clients. This confirms a picture of general disability and longer-term general non-mental health problems adding to problems of mental disorder.

Behavioural aspects appear the least noted aspect in grounds and this contrasts with the position in the rank order of problems (placed 4th against 9th) however <u>vulnerability</u> and <u>family relationships</u> themes reflect the problem data significantly, but proposals for management planning might be regarded as relatively low given that grounds are the basis for a request for powers of management.

When the content and relative number of references on each theme deriving from medical and welfare sources is compared, the picture is as we would expect. Welfare grounds, although fewer in number (114 to 210 in the 1988 cases), in terms of content cover a wider range of more general topics.

Survey of Guardianship Cases 1988

Section 4: Powers of Guardians

The survey recorded information on powers only if there was evidence on file that the power was actively being applied.

The powers reported as being used in the 81 cases were as follows. It should be noted that more than one power may be applied in any individual case.

Table 14   APPLICATION OF STATUTORY POWERS

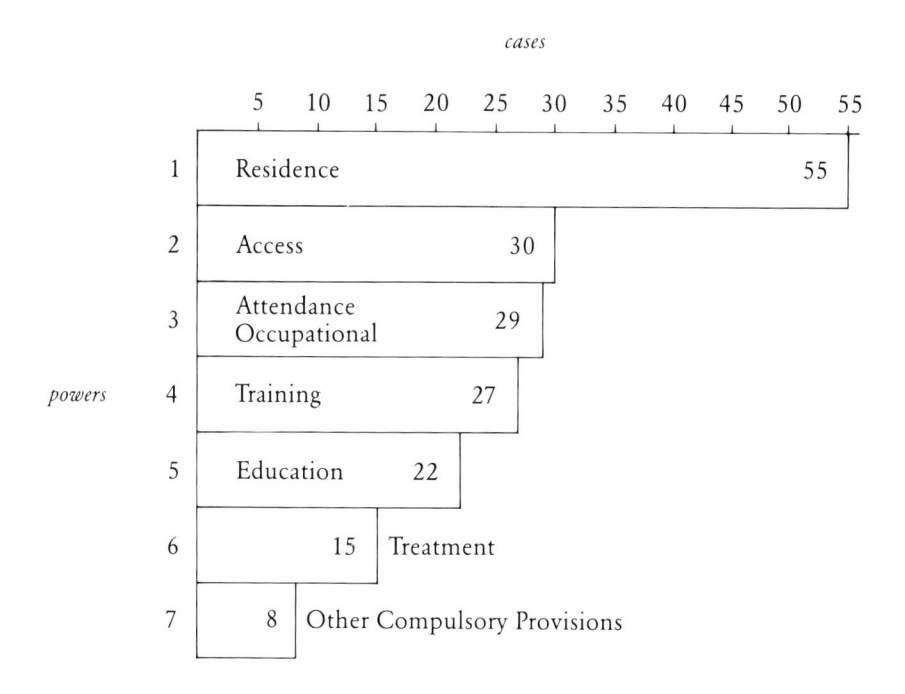

cases

powers		
1	Residence	55
2	Access	30
3	Attendance Occupational	29
4	Training	27
5	Education	22
6	Treatment	15
7	Other Compulsory Provisions	8

68% of people on guardianship in 1988 were required to reside in a particular place, and access to the group, wherever residing, was considered to require enforcement in 37% of instances. The power to require attendance is clearly being utilised for occupation, training, education and treatment.

Guardianship

In the light of the data on powers per person and below with only 11% not being subject to some statutory requirements, most clients are likely to be required to attend day time activities. The concentration of the use of the powers in particular cases can be seen in the following table:

Table 15   POWERS PER PERSON

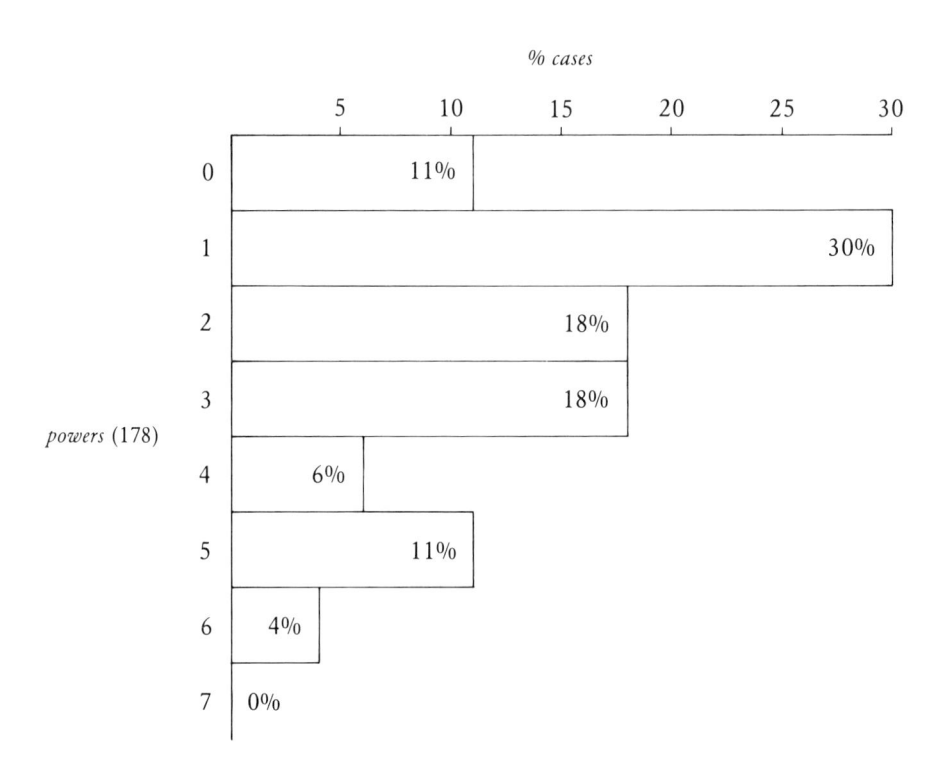

powers (178)

powers	% cases
0	11%
1	30%
2	18%
3	18%
4	6%
5	11%
6	4%
7	0%

11% of those on guardianship required no exercise of powers. This may be because they were benefiting from the protection and services which guardianship provides. However 89% of those on guardianship were subject to the use and therefore the constraints of the powers. We have already seen that the most commonly used single power is that of 'residence' but that this is matched by the combined totals of requirement to "attend" for various reasons. At the other extreme an equal number 11% of clients required the exercise of 5 of the powers. In total those requiring the exercise of 4 or more of the 6 powers totalled 21%. Therefore more than 1 in 5 of those subject to guardianship (17 clients in 81) require intervention, control and/or protection in a comprehensive way that spans residence, attendance and access.

There were therefore 178 reports of the use of statutory powers under guardianship in 81 cases in 1988 and an average of two powers per client with only 11% of clients not actively subject to statutory powers.

It is a matter for further exploration given the data on the low numbers of 'named' guardians as to how local authority employees (social worker or mental health officer) or parental guardians exercise discretion on the application of a power and how it is enforced.

The 1988 survey shows that the client group subject to guardianship did require a significant use of the statutory powers. Other studies currently underway may show cases which were considered unsuitable for guardianship either because the forms of statutory intervention were considered to be an unnecessary infringement of the person's rights or by contrast where the powers were considered as likely to be ineffective because of the lack of powers of enforcement.

The evidence from this study points to the need for and actual application of powers to intervene on a short-term basis, to protect on a longer term basis and to require significant number of cases to reside in a particular place and to attend day time activities including treatment.

Survey of Guardianship Cases 1988

Section 5: Services Received by People on Guardianship

The 81 cases were receiving assistance from 16 kinds of services and a total of 361 contacts with such services were reported, an average of 4.4 per client.

The services used were as follows:

Table 16 SERVICES USED BY PEOPLE ON GUARDIANSHIP

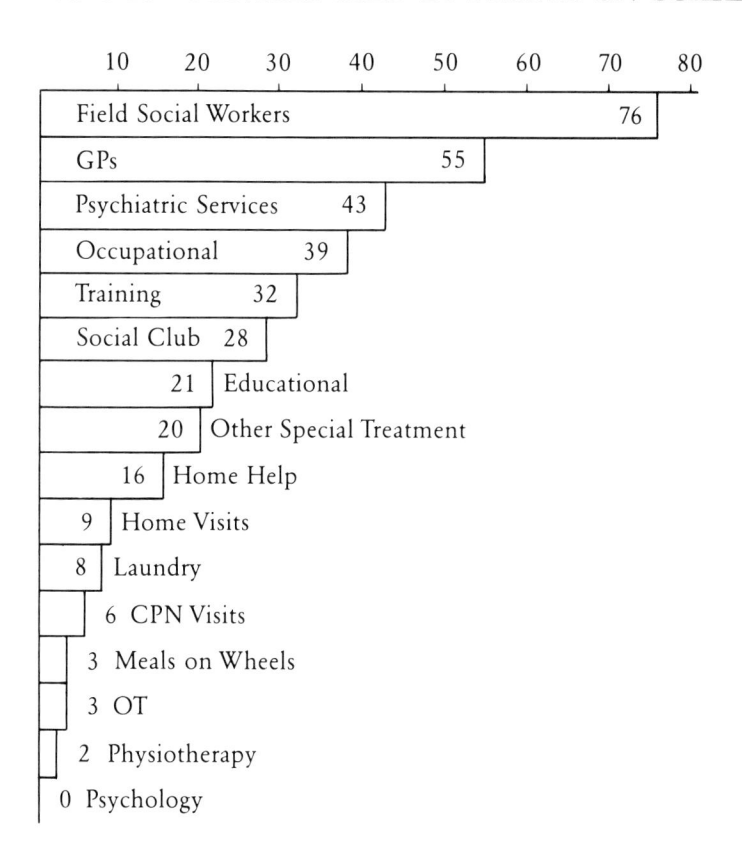

Service	Count
Field Social Workers	76
GPs	55
Psychiatric Services	43
Occupational	39
Training	32
Social Club	28
Educational	21
Other Special Treatment	20
Home Help	16
Home Visits	9
Laundry	8
CPN Visits	6
Meals on Wheels	3
OT	3
Physiotherapy	2
Psychology	0

Guardianship

There appeared to be 5 cases not in regular contact with a Social Work Department and 26 cases not in contact with primary Health Care. 53% of the group were in contact with Psychiatric Services but none in contact with Psychological Services which in the light of reported educational problems in Section 2 is of note.

Use of day time activities such as occupation, education and training confirms the figures on the use of compulsory powers in these areas, with the small increase shown in use of these services being by those not required to use them.

Nearly a quarter of the group use other specialist medical services apart from GP and psychiatric services and this reflects the significant level of non-mental health problems shown in the 'problems' section.

There are a group of domiciliary services, home help, home visiting, community psychiatric nursing visits, meals on wheels and laundry services being used at a relatively low level.

To this data on services must be added information on those using residential facilities, from the housing/accommodation data in Table 5 Section 1.

The full picture of service use by those on guardianship is therefore as follows:

Services used by People on Guardianship

Table 17

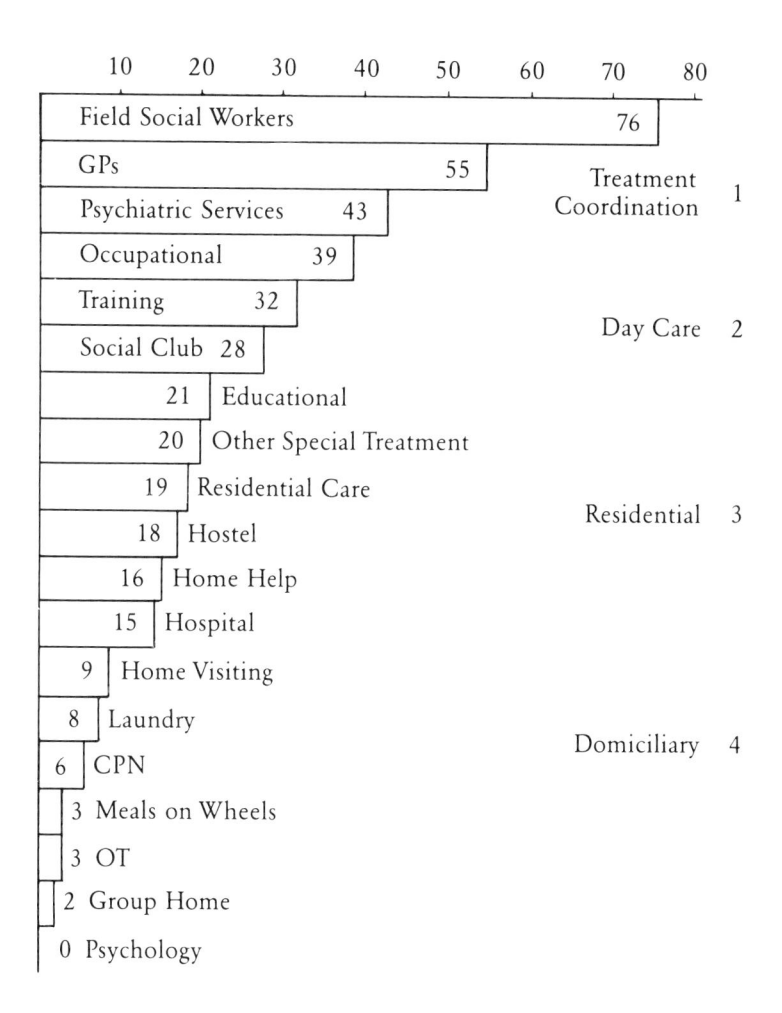

Service	Count	Category	
Field Social Workers	76	Treatment Coordination	1
GPs	55		
Psychiatric Services	43		
Occupational	39	Day Care	2
Training	32		
Social Club	28		
Educational	21		
Other Special Treatment	20		
Residential Care	19	Residential	3
Hostel	18		
Home Help	16		
Hospital	15		
Home Visiting	9	Domiciliary	4
Laundry	8		
CPN	6		
Meals on Wheels	3		
OT	3		
Group Home	2		
Psychology	0		

In this table "service use" can be considered not only in terms of the type and volume of services currently used but also the likely future pattern of service use. Future assessment for service is likely to show significant demand for day time/care activities and for residential facilities.

The current pattern of service use would suggest that for this group of clients, assessed needs will be for services in the following areas as shown on Table 17.

1. Care Coordination
   Specific treatment

2. Day Time Activity
   Occupation and Training

3. Residential Services
   Hospital admission when necessary

4. Domiciliary Services
   Management of funds

Significantly also is the fact that 84% of those on guardianship are single with less than 10% having ever married. This suggests that there will be few carers or close family available to support these people in years to come. Continuity of an established domestic setting may also be infrequent since in the 1988 guardianship cases only 7.5%, 6 people lived in their own home. We can therefore add a 5th area of service need which could be classified as "social support".

Section 6: Management of Funds

The Act Section 41(3) proscribes the "intromitting" by guardians of wards funds. From the problems section we know that 68% of the group were regarded as suffering from financial management problems with 11% being regarded as vulnerable to exploitation. The survey sought to obtain information on formal and informal fund management.

Formal arrangements were in place in 29 cases, 7 were cases of Curator Bonis (8.6%) and an "appointee" could be identified in 22 cases (27%).

Self management of funds was relatively high at 47%, nearly half the group.

Therefore 36% had formal curatory or appointeeship against a background of high levels of problems in money management at 68%.

Informal management of funds occurred in 88% of cases (71), in most cases fund management was undertaken by residential staff for those in such care, family members undertook the task in 15 cases with 'others' in 13. Social workers undertook fund management in 5 cases and guardians themselves in 10 instances (12%). These categories overlap in that residential care workers, families, guardians may be reported as appointees.

The overall picture is of the requirements for assistance in the management of funds being fulfilled by a variety of persons, some in formal roles.

Guardianship

Table 18 MANAGEMENT OF FUNDS

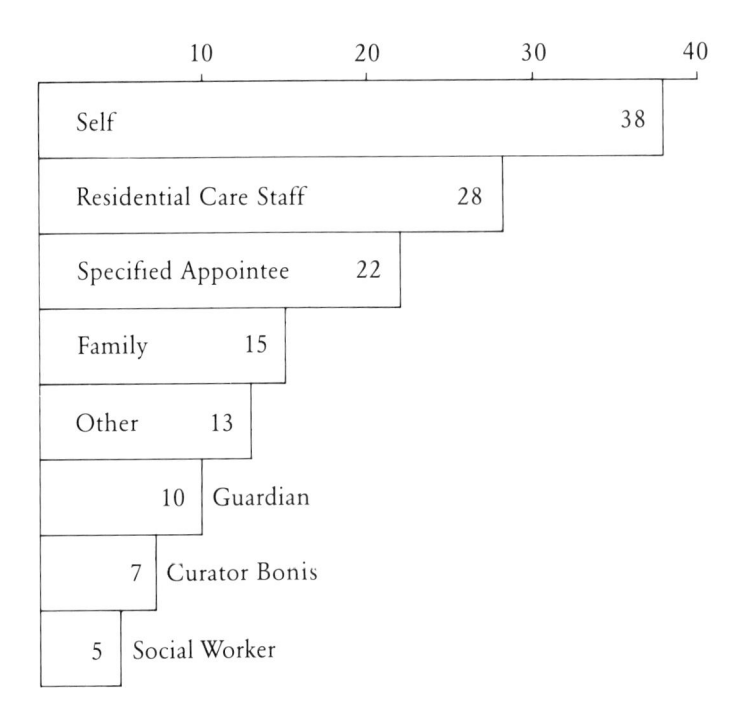

Self	38
Residential Care Staff	28
Specified Appointee	22
Family	15
Other	13
Guardian	10
Curator Bonis	7
Social Worker	5

Section 7: Court Hearings, Orders for Discharge and Complaints

23 (28%) of the 81 1988 cases had been the subject of a Sheriff Court Hearing. One in 4 (11) had been contested. These cases were contested by relatives in 5 cases, patients in 3 and by 'others' in 3.

In short just over a quarter of cases in 1988 were subject to a court Hearing and about half of those were contested. We do not have data on successfully contested guardianship applications but of the 81 cases surveyed 70 proceeded without objection. This does not, however, imply consent or cooperation on the part of the ward or the relatives and the active use of statutory powers suggests that intervention is probably without the full agreement of those subject to the provisions.

In the 1988 group there were 9 requests for discharge by clients and none were upheld.

The turnover of guardianship cases is however not determined to any significant extent by requests for discharge to the Commission, however, the survey did show that 41 cases required further action by the Commission in terms of further investigation under Section 3(2)(a) of the Mental Health (Scotland) Act. This suggests that 50% of guardianship cases will require action at any point and given the turnover data of nearly half the 81 cases in 1988 by termination (20) and new cases (26) a significant enquiry and monitoring function is required. This is confirmed by the 1991 figures which show 31 new cases in a total of 71.

There were records of complaints in 27% of 1988 cases (more than 1 in 4 clients).

Guardianship

YEAR END GUARDIANSHIP STATISTICS – BY REGION
1985 - 1991

REGIONS	1985	1986	1987	1988	1989	1990	1991
Strathclyde	—	—	—	—	15	25	24
Lothian	—	—	—	—	9	14	14
Grampian	—	—	—	—	12	12	13
Highland	—	—	—	—	3	5	9
Dumfries & Galloway	—	—	—	—	1	4	4
Central	—	—	—	—	0	2	3
Fife	—	—	—	—	1	1	0
Shetland	—	—	—	—	1	1	1
Tayside	—	—	—	—	3	1	3
TOTAL	61	60	57	61	45	65	71

— = *not available*

GUARDIANSHIP CASES – BY YEAR
1985 - 1990

Year	Cases at start of year	Discharges during years	Approvals during years	Cases at end of years	Total number of cases contacted
1985	73	27	15	61	88
1986	61	12	11	60	82
1987	60	24	21	57	81
1988	57	23	27	61	84
1989	61	31	14	45	75
1990	45	19	39	65	84

CHAPTER 4

Historical Background and Survey

We have considered the historical evolution of guardianship in a social and legal context, and drawn together the practice literature on guardianship. We have described the profile of people on guardianship in the year 1988, highlighting their significant characteristics, individual problems, the grounds for guardianship, the use of powers and their linkage to the provision of services.

What can we learn from this work which can contribute to the ongoing debate on the practice and development of guardianship? It is not our remit to develop detailed proposals, rather to point to themes for further discussion. The recent publication of the Scottish Law Commission Discussion Paper 94 on legislation in relation to mentally disabled adults provides us with that opportunity. However we should bear in mind that new legislation may be a number of years away and we have an immediate concern to ensure that current policy and practice in guardianship is sustained and developed.

History reveals the movement away from private towards public guardianship. Private guardianship is defined as the ward having a related or non-related person acting as guardian and normally residing with that person, and public guardianship is defined as the ward, regardless of where he/she is living, having a local authority employee as guardian. Guardianship has its roots in, and overlapped with boarding-out in the pre 1913 period. It operated predominantly on a private basis but with steadily falling numbers throughout the sixties and seventies until the Mental Health (Scotland) Act was amended in 1984.

The Local Authority as Guardian

The local authority as guardian is now the central feature of practice under the 1984 Act and some argue that the role has been professionalised and made less personal. The multiple needs, vulnerability and dependency of the clients in our survey would suggest that a balance should be struck between

Guardianship

professional public guardians and lay private guardians. The trend towards use of public or local authority guardians is attributable to a number of factors:

1. welfare state benefit provisions no longer requiring formal guardianship to ensure income for the person requiring care within a private household.

2. changing professional attitudes about how persons with mental disorder should be managed, for example in the least restrictive and as normal an environment as possible.

3. the absence of a procedure whereby the suitability of someone applying to be a private guardian can be assessed.

In the current climate of the predominance of public guardians, evaluating this trend is hindered by the low number of cases and also by the impression that guardianship has not received the social work profession's best attention with the result that its advantages for clients have not been fully developed.

Placement and Costs of Care

Our historical review also provides additional perspectives on some current social policy problems. The early distinction made by Inspectors of the Poor between "paupers" and "lunatics" as regards access to, and costs of different forms of care, poorhouse or asylum, exercise us today in new ways. As increasing numbers of more dependent persons are placed in the community the distinction between health and social care components, and where costs fall, may contribute to a reluctance of local authorities to develop their role as public guardians for such people. When lay, private guardians were numerous they provided personal care in a regulated and publically financed form of boarding out. It may be that personal private guardians may require remuneration to offer such a service today, in the form of a carer's allowance or by "brokered" purchase of service by the ward from income and benefits.

It is also of note that the community care provision of boarding out was seen as a way of restricting asylum building. The decline of guardianship in

Scotland in the 60s and 70s coincided with continuing admissions of people with mental handicap to hospital so that by the mid 80s, guardianship cases had declined to 61 and 40% of all hospitalised mentally handicapped people in Scotland lived in two large institutions. A survey at that time estimated that significant numbers of such people would be more appropriately placed in the community.

Care, Control and Risk

Under the proposals now put forward by the Scottish Law Commission the new style personal guardianship "would not be slanted towards local authority guardianship". One of the themes in the forthcoming debate will, therefore, be in this area of private or public guardianship which has clear-sounding echoes of the past.

A recurring theme in any debate on guardianship is the balance of care and control. History reveals this as an unbroken thread woven into the fabric of legislation and management through the years. Care is related to dependency, vulnerability, compassion, social justice, corporate and personal responsibility; control is related to intervention, fear, social order, public and personal threat, and sometimes stigma.

Care and control converge in the assessment of risk to vulnerable and dependent people. Care and control may also extend beyond the person subject to guardianship to his/her circumstances of family, estate, health and social nexus. Any system of guardianship has to look to meeting need within a balance of such factors.

The literature reviewed gave illustrations of care and raised matters such as resources for persons on guardianship, professional uncertainty in workers, the poor take-up of guardianship in relation to protecting vulnerable people, the applicability of guardianship to the elderly and offenders. It also illustrated questions about control in raising matters such as the lack of sanctions, the vagueness of powers, absence of authority to treat and reluctance to use guardianship as a restriction.

Our survey amply revealed the risk factors in the lives of 81 people on guardianship and the use being made of both care and control to meet their welfare needs.

The Scottish Law Commission's Discussion Paper emphasises the importance of having two core principles observed in any new system, maximising the individual's own faculties and introducing only the control measures needed for care and protection and for the achievement of a quality of life which would be generally accepted as being as normal as possible. The balance of care and control, is central to effective and practical legal arrangements for managing mentally disordered adults.

Practice Guidance

It is clear both from our historical review and the survey that policy and operational practice of local authority social work departments exercise a decisive influence on the applications for and use of guardianship. Local authorities, however, appear to remain ambivalent about its use. Clear policy guidelines have been slow to emerge and published manuals of good practice procedures are few. In broader terms, however, there is an understandable reluctance on the part of local authority social work departments to adopt a general responsibility as guardian for the many mentally handicapped patients returning to the community from hospitals.

The scope of the 1984 Act, in including dementia, mental handicap and mental illness under the term mental disorder targets the guardianship provisions on a wide and highly differential set of client groups.

The lack of practice guidance in relation to the distinctive application of guardianship to the three client groups has, coupled to the reluctance of local authorities to promote the provision, resulted in a generalised and vague grasp of the effective use of the specific enabling powers.

The significant decline in the personal named guardian has also turned emphasis within guardianship towards the use of powers and provision of services rather than to a relationship with a personal guardian.

Further practice problems arise when the exercise of a power under mental health guardianship creates further compulsion. In the case of the requirement to reside, payment may have to be made for residence by the ward. Residence in hospital entails the acceptance of treatment as nursing care. Not all controls contingent upon guardianship have been sufficiently discussed in terms of good practice.

The problem of balancing care and control issues sometimes leads to inaction. It is not uncommon to encounter an objection to the use of guardianship based on its curtailment of a client's civil rights being stated alongside an objection which points to the practical difficulties of enforcement and the inadequacies of the powers.

There are also fears about the resource implications of allocating field workers' time to an increasing number of guardianship cases.

Care - Management

There have been other inhibiting factors in the use of guardianship. The co-ordination of applications to the Sheriff Court, lack of clarity of who should be named as guardian, and absence of specified powers or sanctions have all been factors reported as discouraging use.

The co-ordination (care-management) of guardianship has not emerged as a basis for ongoing specialist Mental Health Officer work and their tasks are frequently of an administrative nature surrounding applications and renewals. Even in the latter activity, unplanned terminations of guardianship are only now being addressed by creating registers of cases in some local authorities.

Since the enactment of the National Health Service and Community Care legislation there has been a further focus on the relationship between being a guardian and providing services on an assessed basis. This has sharpened the debate about whether those under guardianship of the local authority should have access to services in a way that differs from other clients.

Local authorities are also concerned to maximise community care provision for the people likely to be subject to guardianship. This entails the search for normal settings for living and occupation. It also suggests an important role for members of the community in such a provision. It remains a matter of speculation, however, as to whether the lay public will be able or willing to come forward and become involved as guardians for the dependent and sometimes disturbed clients described in our survey. Potential guardians may also be deterred by the difficulties they may encounter in negotiating with local authorities and professional persons for services for their wards.

Personal Guardianship

Turning to consider the opportunity afforded by the Scottish Law Commission Discussion Paper 94, it seems appropriate to consider the new proposals in the light of our conclusions. It should be noted that the Mental Welfare Commission will produce further detailed responses in 1992.

There seems little doubt that the unease and criticism from policy makers in local authorities, social workers and the Mental Welfare Commission about guardianship supports the proposal that there should be a new system of personal guardianship introduced.

The Scottish Law Commission has asked for views on moving away from a local authority dominated guardianship system and canvasses the possibility that a guardian should be a family member or have a close personal relationship with the disabled person.

Our survey showed that one of the commoner reasons for persons being placed on guardianship was problematic family relationships and it seems likely that none of the 83 per cent with such problems could have readily had "a family member" as a guardian. In many instances it was the family which presented the main threat to the disabled person and as long as this continues as a feature of the lives of persons being considered for guardianship, there will be a significant number of people who will require "a professional guardian". Perhaps it can be argued that in the absence of suitable family members, lay people can be found to develop "close personal relationships" but this raises questions about whether such people will come forward; what system for vetting their suitability will be required; what financial and other support they receive; how they perceive their relationship with specialist services, and how they can obtain appropriate resources when needed. Will non-local authority personal guardians be able to command resources on behalf of their ward? This of course has to be asked bearing in mind the provisions of the National Health Service and Community Care Act which should enable provision of services. It remains to be seen whether non-professionals will be able to master the intricacies of the procedures.

If the local authority becomes the public guardian of last resort in cases where no family member or relative can be identified as a guardian or where special or complex problems exist then the close personal relationship may be created with a named professional guardian. Whilst this may assist in access to needed services for the more complex cases the potential for a two tier system may be created. The two tiers may not so much reflect the assessed complexities of cases as the extent of family problems; absence of suitable lay personal guardians and the socio-economic position of these families.

Fund Management

The management of a mentally disordered person's finances, estate or property, has always been linked with guardianship. History shows that the origins of guardianship were property based. Fiscal matters have strongly influenced what kind of care individuals have received when suffering from mental disorder both in terms of the financing of care and in the management of the ward's finances and capacity for self-management.

Our survey shows that financial problems were present in 83 per cent of the 1988 guardianship cases yet current guardianship legislation specifically prohibits intromitting with patients' funds. The Scottish Law Commission proposals cover financial management and are likely to result in considerable clarification in this area.

Criteria for Guardianship: Incapacity and Welfare

The need to establish welfare grounds for guardianship was introduced by the 1984 Act and is frequently referred to in the literature on guardianship.

The principle of establishing welfare grounds appears to be valued, but the methods and criteria are less clear, highlighting the need for and the importance of guidance in assessing welfare grounds. There has been a recognition that evaluating risk factors and working with a concept of incapacity are complex areas.

Uncertainty amongst Mental Health Officers about the interface between mental state and welfare risks emerged in the Edinburgh University Study and in our survey reference by MHOs to mental state in the welfare grounds to court was common.

Incapacity, or partial incapacity and welfare are closely linked but practice in the field may be assisted by making a number of distinctions

The functional assessment of individuals in their social context is related to but distinct from a medical or legal definition of incapacity. A critical issue in the forthcoming debate on the future provisions for guardianship will be whether welfare grounds based on an assessment of risk, consideration of functional capacity and even the wishes of the prospective ward will be central to the process of placing people on guardianship, or whether guardianship might be considered in cases of incapacity or potential incapacity as defined in a medico-legal sense. The balance that can be struck between these necessary components for guardianship will influence the way in which the ward's problems are defined and the part to be played by applicants and subsequently carers and welfare agencies.

The proposals in Discussion Paper 94 do not advocate maintaining the current welfare grounds as such and propose that the appointing body should be satisfied that the person in question lacks wholly or partly the capacity to understand the nature of and to foresee possible implications of personal welfare decisions and that the personal guardian would result in a substantial benefit to or necessary protection of, the person.

This raises the question as to whether a new system would be most effective if it included the existing "welfare grounds" supported by developed guidelines on assessment, alongside the requirement for partial incapacity in, both a medico-legal and a social and functional sense.

Conclusion

The current debate on guardianship within the context of decision-making for mentally incapacitated adults and its relation to fund management provide an opportunity to:

- establish a new balance between public and private guardians
- clarify the legal status of wards
- be specific about powers of care and control conferred on guardians
- include both cognitive and functional aspects of capacity and their relationship through guardianship to welfare benefit
- create ease of access to such a framework via courts or Tribunals or Hearings

It is the Mental Welfare Commission's hope that this publication, which brings a historical perspective, an account of problems in practice and a census of Scottish guardianship cases, will contribute to a thorough debate alongside the Scottish Law Commission's recent publication.